The Danish Chair
– An International Affair

'S Strandberg Publishing

The book is published with
the support of the following
foundations

Augustinus Fonden
dreyersfond

**DESIGN
MUSEUM
DANMARK**

Christian Holmsted Olesen

the danish chair

an international affair

Content

7 ——— A visual book on chairs

16 ——— Folding stools and chairs
36 ——— Low easy chairs
56 ——— Peasant chairs
78 ——— Bentwood chairs
106 ——— Chinese chairs
132 ——— Frame chairs
176 ——— English chairs
202 ——— Windsor chairs
224 ——— Shell chairs
292 ——— Cantilever chairs

325 ——— Danish furniture designers who shaped their field

335 ——— Literature

The chair is a very difficult object. Everyone who has ever tried to make one knows that. There are endless possibilities and many problems – the chair has to be light, it has to be strong, it has to be comfortable. It is almost easier to build a skyscraper than a chair.

— Ludwig Mies van der Rohe

A visual book on chairs

In 2016, Designmuseum Danmark opened the permanent exhibition The Danish Chair – An International Affair. The idea behind the exhibition, which was created in collaboration with the designer Boris Berlin, is to display 113 of the museum's chairs like gemstones in jewellery chests or individually framed, presented as the works of art that they are. Without the use of words, solely by visual means, the exhibition aims to tell the story of what is perhaps the most defining quality of Danish 20th-century chair design: the way the chairs relate to each other and to chair forms and concepts from previous eras and foreign cultures.

The book pursues the same ambition. By moving through the pages and using their eyes, readers should be able to gain an understanding of how the so-called Golden Age of Danish furniture design was shaped by the study and refinement of historical furniture types. It shows the family relations between the chairs and how they inspired each other conceptually and with regard to specific details and constructions.

The book thus offers a visual introduction to the topic of the Danish chair in the 20th century. Readers interested in knowing more about the chairs' design process, context, life, success and so forth can turn to the list of recommended reading in the back of the book.

**Designmuseum Danmark
– a vital hub in the development of Danish Design**

The book deals exclusively with chairs from the collections of Designmuseum Danmark, and this small selection of 113 chairs provides an insight into the museum's vital role in the development of the concept of Danish Design. The modern notion of design emerged with industrialisation, and the Great Exhibition in London in 1851 is often mentioned as its specific origin. In the wake of the exhibition, the Victoria and Albert Museum, the world's first museum for applied art or arts and crafts, was conceived as a museum with collections of the finest objects from all ages and cultures with the goal of enlightening the public and stimulating their sense of quality while also inspiring industry to manufacture better products. Attached to the museum were schools charged with training future designers based on studies of the past.

As a new museum type, the arts and crafts museum, the *Kunstgewerbemuseum* or, in Danish, the *kunstindustrimuseum*, now designmuseum, spread across Europe during the second half of the 20th century. This new development sprang from the historicist movement, which was driven by an affinity for the past. The modernist breakthrough in the early 20th century was driven by a desire to break with tradition; rather than looking to the past, the future should be based on new technologies and scientific research. Thus, in many countries, the new museums did not come to play a major role in the development of contemporary design.

Denmark was one of the last European countries to establish a Museum of Art & Design in 1890 (now Designmuseum Danmark), but in a sense, it became the most accomplished of its kind in Europe as a vital hub in the development of design culture in Denmark throughout the 20th century. Unlike the modernists in most countries, Danish designers based their work on tradition and history, which they translated into something new, a Danish style that had its international breakthrough around 1950 under the labels of Danish Design and Danish Modern. Over the past 125 years, most Danish designers have made good use of the collections of Designmuseum Danmark, and many of the best-known Danish design icons are based on historical models from the museum's collections.

Denmark is known in particular for its furniture culture, but the country has a long tradition for excellent and highly developed craftsmanship within many areas. As Denmark has no raw materials, agriculture has historically been the country's main source of income. Industrialisation reached Denmark fairly late and did not really gain momentum until after the Second World War. During the early 1920s the many skilled Copenhagen cabinetmakers felt the competition from German furniture manufacturers that had begun to sell industrially produced quality furniture in Denmark. In response, the cabinetmakers joined forces, and in 1927 they began to stage annual exhibitions to showcase what they had to offer. The Copenhagen Cabinetmakers' Guild exhibitions continued until 1966 and were a major event in Copenhagen, and they were held at Designmuseum Danmark.

During the 1930s, the cabinetmakers began to partner with furniture designers to create new pieces for the exhibitions. Each cabinetmaker had a running collaboration with a specific designer, and from 1933, design competitions became a regular part of the annual exhibitions, which played a vital role in the development of Danish furniture culture during the 20th century. Close to half of the Danish furniture classics were designed for the Guild exhibitions, and many of these models were later modified for industrial production. The exhibitions were visited by the general public and engaged wide swathes of society in a critical debate about the interiors and furnishing of future homes, thus serving as a laboratory where cabinetmakers and furniture designers could test their experiments on the public.

For innovative modernist designers, the Guild exhibitions were an opportunity for showing the public how to create a better, more usage-oriented, democratic and socially responsible housing culture, and the furniture designers' work thus contributed to the development of the socially oriented welfare state. Most 20th-century Danish designers, not just furniture designers, had a craft background. Applicants to the School of Arts and Crafts, which was located at Designmuseum Danmark, had to have a certificate of apprenticeship. As a result, Danish design has always been based on the virtues of good craftsmanship with its emphasis on natural, sensuous and tactile materials, perfect joints and detailing and tried and tested, simple constructions.

In this old Protestant peasant culture that was never particularly wealthy, thrift and optimal use of material resources have always been second nature, a feature that was well aligned with the minimalism characterising international modernism. Politically, Denmark had not seen revolutions, and the same applies to design history. Denmark is known for learning from other countries and taking a common-sense view of trends and new, promising ideas, refining and cultivating them. Thus, 'unpretentious', 'understated' and 'subtle' are some of the terms commonly used to describe the simple and carefully considered Danish design. And while international modernism posited 'form follows function' as the goal of the utilitarian design of the new era, the Danish architect Professor Kay Fisker spoke of 'the functional tradition', arguing that Danish design has always been user-centred and practised with the inclusion of regional materials and traditions.

Architect, Professor Steen Eiler Rasmussen argued that Danish design was simply more functionalist than Central European design. He wrote about the work of Professor of Furniture Kaare Klint:

'One might say that Kaare Klint aimed for practical efficiency, while contemporary European modernism strove for stylistic impact.'

Rasmussen argued that because Danish design sprang from traditional tool design it was more usage-oriented than, for example, the new Bauhaus school, which had a stronger production focus in its celebration of industrialisation. Danish design was not widely characterised by new or innovative ideas but was more pragmatic in nature. Simplicity, an austere colour range, quality materials and an affinity for tradition were in fact less of a deliberate choice and more of a necessity, as good craftsmanship was all there was. The fact that Denmark was lagging behind the development in other Western countries during the early 20th century would prove to be a major advantage in the mid 20th century.

In 1949 many foreign journalists came to Copenhagen to see the Guild exhibition at Designmuseum Danmark. Several of the furniture designers had begun to take a freer approach to the historical models. While Kaare Klint and many of his students had initially pursued a strictly geometric idiom, several designers were now creating more expressive and organic designs, some, including Finn Juhl, under impression of the new organic modernism in art, and others, including Hans J. Wegner, with inspiration from traditional tools, such as axes and oars, whose form was conditioned by their purpose.

American journalists began to write about this organic furniture executed with sublime craftsmanship, and soon, demand for Danish furniture design began to soar in the Western world. The Danish state, together with other Scandinavian countries, seized the opportunity and launched a major marketing campaign for Danish culture and design in Western countries over the following decade, especially in the United States, the United Kingdom and Germany. Several American museums presented travelling exhibitions about Scandinavian design during the 1950s.

The great success of Danish design in the United States after the Second World War stemmed in part from the fact that almost all other countries had abandoned craft-based production in favour of industrial manufacturing during the first half of the 20th century. After the Second World War there was a nostalgic affinity for craft-based products in the United States, a tradition that many tried, less successfully, to revive. Industrialisation was seen to have been instrumental in exacerbating the horrors of the war, since the materiel had been industrially manufactured. At the same time, many of the

Central European modernists had moved to the United States and were influencing the taste and preferences of the American cultural elite. They saw that the Danish variant of modernism lived up to the same requirements of simplicity, functionality, hygiene and honesty that characterised Central European modernism, but that the Danish variant had a more humane, mature and poetic expression. During the 1950s, modernism moved towards more expressive and organic forms, and Danish design was able to contribute to this trend with the design of utilitarian objects, furniture in particular.

One of the exhibits that the American journalists fell for when they visited the Copenhagen Cabinetmakers' Guild exhibition at Designmuseum Danmark in 1949 was Hans J. Wegners Round Chair. They dubbed it The Chair and saw it as the perfect chair. Shortly after the exhibition, cabinetmaker Johannes Hansen received the first order for 400 chairs – he was used to selling a couple of dining room suites at an exhibition. Fortunately, the Danish economy was thriving after the Second World War thanks to the development of the welfare state, and gradually, an industrial sector was developed. In cooperation with the furniture designers, furniture factories such as Fritz Hansen, Salesco and FDB were able to translate many of the qualities and forms of the cabinetmakers' furniture into industrial or semi-industrial manufacturing processes, so that Danish Modern or Danish Design could be exported abroad.

Personally, Wegner was less impressed with The Chair: 'There's nothing new about it, it could have been made 200 years ago.' In a sense, he was right – after all, the chair was based on traditional craft techniques, and it represented a traditional Danish furniture type, a chair with armrests where the top rail embraces the sitter. Although Wegner may not have been aware of the way in which his chair aligned with the spirit of the time, organic modernism, with its elegant and simple-looking curves, he did understand the trend he was a part of when he said, later, 'An extensive process of purification was the basis for the creation of Danish Design.'

In 1989, the Danish architect Keld Vindum wrote in an article in the journal UNDR. Nyt Nordisk Forum (UNDR. New Nordic Forum) titled 'Den store Moderator' (The Great Modifier) that the Danes learn from other countries but refine and cultivate what they import:

'Take the characterisation of the functional tradition as humanised, matured modernism. We almost appear to be compensating for or making a virtue of our inability to come up with something new by insisting that we are the ones making the new ideas usable. We follow others' experiments and filter out what we can use, modify it and use it in our work with what is essential: creating reasonable, carefully thought-out, subtle, modest but highly cultivated items that can be used (…) Tradition, in other words, has become an ideology.'

A chair with a fine lineage

In the late 1920s, Designmuseum Danmark moved into its current location in a former hospital from the 1750s commissioned by King Frederik IV. The architect Kaare Klint had converted the hospital buildings to a museum and created the interior design. He became the first professor of furniture design at the Royal Danish Academy of Fine Arts, School of Architecture and is widely considered the father of modern Danish furniture design. He had a flat at the museum, and his principles came to influence the museum's collection strategy for decades, just as he also shaped the design school, the Furniture School of the School of Arts and Crafts, which was located at the museum. The teachers at the Furniture School were trained by Kaare Klint, and many of the students continued their studies under Klint at the Royal Danish Academy of Fine Arts.

Like other contemporary architects Klint was a functionalist and taught his students that objects should be designed and proportioned for their intended purpose. Nevertheless, he rejected the international modernism that was pursued in Central Europe, because he felt that it was 'throwing the baby out with the bathwater' when, for example, Bauhaus in Germany discarded tradition and wanted to set out by analysing a design task completely from scratch. Klint believed that the principal forms of the older furniture types, furniture designed according to its intended purpose, could be useful in the design of tomorrow's furniture. That is why he had his students measure the historical furniture at the Designmuseum, including pieces from China and Britain. They had to learn and understand how the furniture was constructed, distinguish stylistic eras and make precise drawings. The study of historical types and types from other cultures played a key role in the development of new Danish design during the 20th century.

Kaare Klint spoke of a 'chair of fine lineage'. Furniture that had proved its worth for centuries could be adapted to contemporary needs and production methods, a view that was shared by his student Børge Mogensen. The key was to improve, refine and adapt the best historical objects to the contemporary culture. Hence, most Danish furniture contains recognisable archetypes, often from other cultures than the Danish.

No other design culture is as thoroughly founded in the study of types and forms from other ages and cultures, which may seem paradoxical, since Danish Design is simultaneously regarded as one of the most unambiguously national styles and brands in design history. What held such appeal for the export market was the narrative of craftsmanship, region, society and tradition; this stood in contrast to the international modernism, which sought to detach itself from time and place and create anonymous, purely utilitarian objects. The chair should be a machine, said the international modernists. But perhaps, Danish Design is just as international as the international style, precisely because it cultivates international history, good ideas from other cultures and basic manmade forms and archetypes. Perhaps the real reason why Danish Design from the 20th century has remained popular is that it strives to convey something eternally human, and that it makes a virtue of showing the DNA of the archetypes in the new designs. Wegner's popular Wishbone Chair, for example, has recognisable elements of historical chairs from China, Austria (Thonet), European and American peasant culture, British Windsor chairs, Greek *klismos* chairs and so forth. It is a synthesis where most people can find something they recognise.

The international modernists sought to create optimal objects. They aimed for the best reflection of the idea of the chair, detached from history, culture and time. However, many of the international modernists' furniture pieces were closely tied to their time, because they reflected the conditions of the new technology, as exemplified by the tubular-steel furniture.

Despite the intention of avoiding style entirely, Bauhaus and others were in fact designing objects for the new era – in the new international style.

Danish furniture classics are often described as timeless. That is nonsense, too, of course, but Wegner is right that many of the hand-crafted designs could have been made centuries ago. The strong element of craftsmanship, tradition, history and other cultures in Danish design may add to the longevity of the designs. Today, the Danish furniture design approach that Kaare Klint is regarded as the father of has become a method that is embraced also by international designers. British Jasper Morrison and Japanese Naoto Fukusava speak of 'super normal design': design, whose primary purpose is everyday use. They also both seek to adapt and refine quality designs from the past to incorporate them into today's culture.

The most culture-bearing object

For Wegner, The Chair's success remained a life-long challenge. In his own opinion, he had not created the ultimate chair. 'You can always do a better job,' he said, an ambition he pursued in the 500 or so other chairs he designed. In fact, during the 20th century, the Danes became known especially for designing chairs, and although they were very active in this field, they were not the only ones to assign the chair a special role.

'The chair is a very difficult object. Everyone who has ever tried to make one knows that. There are endless possibilities and many problems – the chair has to be light, it has to be strong, it has to be comfortable. It is almost easier to build a skyscraper than a chair,' said the international modernist Ludwig Mies van der Rohe.

The permanent exhibition at Designmuseum Danmark, The Danish Chair – An International Affair. Exhibition design: Boris Berlin.

In Western design history the chair has generally been regarded as the ultimate design task, the designer's touchstone. It might seem a very simple task – a construction that can raise a human body some 42–46 cm above the ground. Why are these simple body-holders so interesting? Wegner offers an answer: 'The chair is the piece of furniture that is closest to human beings. You can give it the personal touch.'

The chair touches and mirrors the body it supports, with arms, legs, a seat and a back. It is anthropomorphic. It lends the sitter status and identity, and it offers designers an expressive potential. The chair's function as body-holder is secondary. Sitting is unnatural and downright unhealthy. It hampers circulation, inhibits mobility and is harmful to the back. Sitting still on a chair is an acquired skill – just consider how hard it is for children. It is not until the industrial age that the chair is associated with work. Historically, the function of the chair is exclusively symbolic, and it is the most culture-bearing object we have created. It says everything about the time and the social context it was created in, and language tells us of the historical significance of the chair:

judge's seat, academic chair, episcopal chair, legislative seat ... cathedra, chair ...

A visual book on chairs

Chairs are instruments that confer power and status to a person. We adopt a particular posture or position when we sit. Cabinet ministers cling to their seats. Historically, the unnatural static position had been the reserve of chieftains or divine figures, who were seated on thrones. Sitting on something exerts control over it, so historical chairs often had lion's feet, which express authority and oppression. In the chairless Japanese society, only the shogun is seated on a stool, while the samurai fight the war.

With the introduction of democracy in antiquity, the chair stopped having a purely ceremonial purpose and became a utilitarian object. The idea of individual chairs for everyone returned during the Renaissance, as the chair gradually began to replace the bench. Totalitarian societies have often preferred benches, but with the individualism brought on by the Enlightenment, individual chairs became the norm. During the first half of the 20th century the chair was characterised as a machine. The intended point may have been that the chair was a body-holder, a supporting construction, but it was also about controlling the new contemporary religion: technology.

During the second half the 20th century, the age of the consumer society, the chair becomes a lifestyle object, closely related to the individual person's identity. With our chair, we tell the world who we are, fashioning our self-presentation. Designers make chairs for all sorts of people, and the chair becomes an image of the advance of Western democracy. John F. Kennedy was seated in Hans J. Wegner's The Chair during his debate with Richard M. Nixon in 1960, the first televised Presidential debate in history. This was later interpreted as a sign that Kennedy wanted to be associated with the egalitarian ideals, welfare and democracy that the Scandinavian countries represented. In fact, the owner of the TV station hosting the debate was a collector of Danish furniture. However, it was an apt point: the American elite associated the many different Danish chairs with freedom, equality and wealth for all, a reflection of Scandinavian post-war societies.

The matured and humane Danish modernism people talked about was based on natural materials, a life in harmony with nature, based on handed-down traditions. This affinity for traditional form, classic furniture types, illustrated that the old symbols of social status could live on as new poetry with new meanings in the new, democratic world order. This play with historical concepts and forms made Danish modernism resistant to the postmodernist criticism of modernism. Unlike the international style, Danish furniture design could not be criticised as unimaginative, ahistorical and dispassionate rationalism. Although the furniture was sensible and usage-oriented, it was rich in storytelling; it was in fact a sophisticated, simplified continuation of 19th-century historicism, a cultivation of historical forms. Perhaps it was this cultivation of the official symbols of power and the multicultural aspect of Danish furniture design that made it seem exemplary to those who believed in equality, individuality, freedom and democracy after the Second World War.

Presidential candidate John F. Kennedy seated in Hans J. Wegner's Round Chair (see page 160) just before his debate with Richard M. Nixon in 1960, the first televised presidential debate in history.

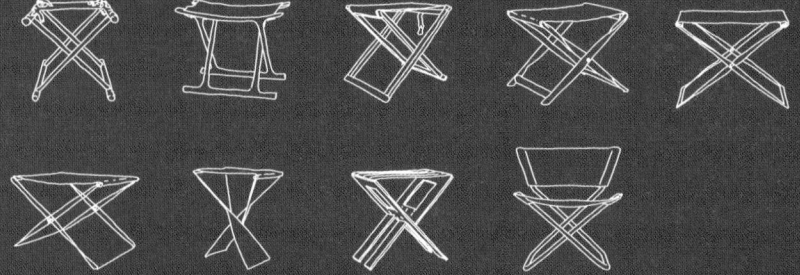

Folding stools and chairs

The X is the simplest of all graphic symbols, and in many ancient cultures the folding chair or stool has been a symbol of power: the seated person commands greater dignity than the standing person. The first folding stool was the general's portable seat. Later, the motif has been repeated in the judge's seat, the Roman official's seat (the curule seat), the Catholic episcopal seat and the royal seat.

The earliest known X-frame chairs are from the Sumerian civilisation in Babylonia, dating from ca. 2600 BC. Images of X-chairs have been found in Cretan/Mycenaean culture dating from ca. 2000–1500 BC, and Egyptian folding stools from ca. 2000–1300 BC have been preserved. The oldest Danish folding stool is the ca. 3.000-year-old ash stool from the Guldhøj (Gold Hill) barrow by Vamdrup, which is now in the National Museum of Denmark. It probably belonged to a nobleman who was buried along with the stool and his bronze weapons. It resembles the Egyptian types – Danish furniture design has long been drawing on inspiration from abroad.

18 —— Japanese folding stool
20 —— Folding stool, Ole Wanscher
22 —— MK99220, Mogens Koch
24 —— Propeller folding stool, Kaare Klint
26 —— EKC91, Poul Kjærholm
28 —— Folding stool, Jørgen Gammelgaard
30 —— Propeller folding stool, Jørgen Gammelgaard
32 —— Folding stool, Stig Herman Olsen
34 —— Z-Down, Erik Magnussen

Japanese folding stool

Japan

year: 1580–1600
materials: Wood, lacquer, bronze
inv. no.: 182/1987

The first known X-frame chairs were made by the Sumerians in Babylon around 2600 BC. Images of X-chairs have been found in Cretan/Mycenaean culture dating from 2000–1500 BC. In several ancient cultures, folding stools and chairs were a symbol of power. A seated person commands greater dignity than someone standing. The folding chair evolved as a portable seat for a general. The concept is repeated in the judge's seat, the Roman official's chair (the curule seat), the Catholic episcopal chair and the royal throne. This Japanese stool belonged to the furniture historian and designer Ole Wanscher and was a military commander's chair.

Folding stool

Ole Wanscher
1903–1985

year: 1957
materials: Rosewood, leather
prod. by: A.J. Iversen
inv. no.: 151/1958

The oldest item of furniture in Denmark is the ca. 3,000-year-old folding ash chair from the Guldhøj (Gold Hill) barrow near Vamdrup, which is now in the National Museum of Denmark. Folding stools from Egypt from 2000–1300 BC have also been preserved.

Professor Ole Wanscher made an in-depth study of the folding chair. He measured older stools and researched their history, and both wrote and lectured on the history of the folding chair. His measurements revealed great similarities between the Guldhøj chair and the ancient Egyptian stools. The design of the stool he designed for the 1957 Copenhagen Cabinetmakers' Guild Exhibition at the Danish Museum of Art & Design (now Designmuseum Danmark) was based on the measurements of an Egyptian stool from the 15th–13th centuries BC.

MK99220

Mogens Koch
1898–1992

year: 1960
materials: Beech, canvas
prod. by: Interna
inv. no.: 78/2016

Mogens Koch was a professor of architecture rather than of furniture design, but he studied under Kaare Klint, and his contribution to furniture design was highly significant. Like Klint, he was intrigued by rational proportions, and his historical research focused on figures and geometry. He tackled the folding concept in much of his furniture: tables, chairs and, of course, the humble little folding stool. Its almost anonymous, but wonderfully conceived look is typical of Koch. The stool has been a permanent fixture in Designmuseum Danmark's exhibitions for a number of years.

Propeller folding stool

Kaare Klint
1888–1954

year: 1930
materials: Ash, canvas
prod. by: Rud. Rasmussens Snedkerier
inv. no.: 310/2004

There were four Professors of Furniture Design at the Royal Danish Academy of Fine Arts in Copenhagen: Kaare Klint, Ole Wanscher, Poul Kjærholm and Jørgen Gammelgaard. Each one of them tackled the oldest of all seats: the folding stool.

Professor Klint was obsessed with mathematics and wanted to create furniture that could fold and form a whole. When folded, the legs of his stool constitute two poles. The original idea was for the two side frames to curve out from a single pole, but this proved unfeasible. The saw blade removes so much wood that the two pieces would not form a pole after the process. That is why he used a separate piece of wood for each leg.

The 1964 Copenhagen Cabinetmakers' Guild's furniture exhibition.

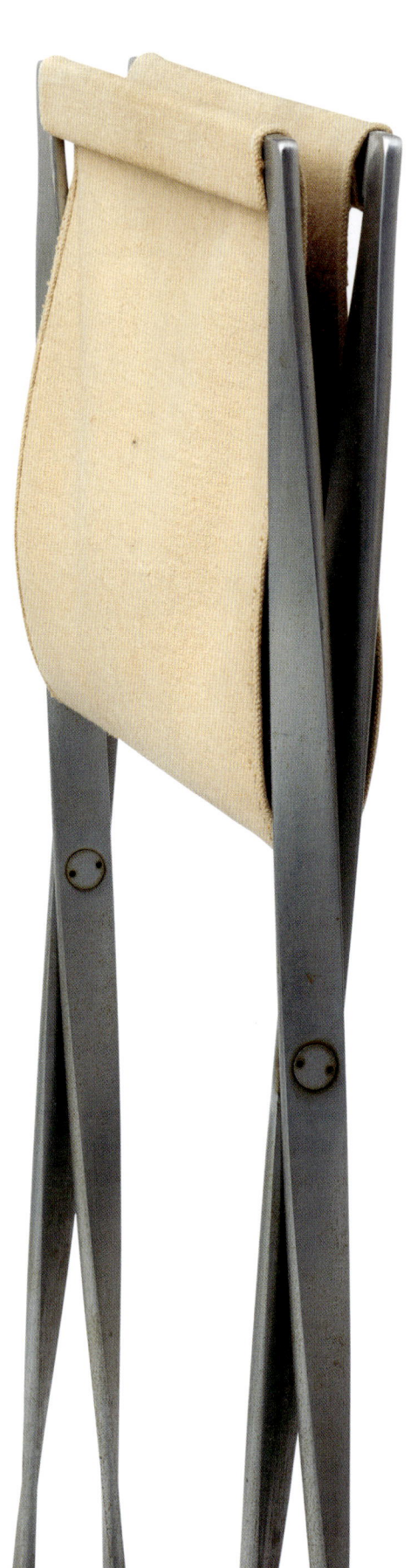

EKC91

Poul Kjærholm
1929–1980

year:	1961–1962
materials:	Chromed flat steel, Pomeranian canvas
prod. by:	E. Kold Christensen
inv. no.:	11/1963

Professor Poul Kjærholm, who translated the Danish carpentry tradition into flat steel, took up the propeller concept that had emerged in Klint's work with poles (see page 24). While the stool ended up looking much lighter than Klint's, it is actually fairly heavy.

Exhibition at Mobilier International, Paris 1965.

Folding stools and chairs | **EKC91** – Poul Kjærholm

Folding stool

Jørgen Gammelgaard
1938–1991

year: 1970
materials: Metal, nylon
prod. by: Johannes Hansen
inv. no.: 63/1970

Professor Jørgen Gammelgaard was interested in industrial materials and often worked with pipe constructions. In his wire version of the propeller stool he competes with Klint (see page 24) and Kjærholm (see page 26) on visual lightness. Gammelgaard's stool is permeated by space to a much higher degree.

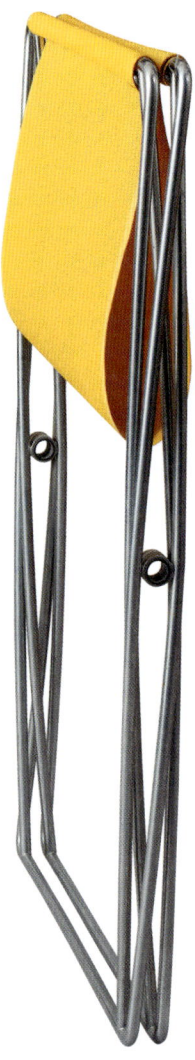

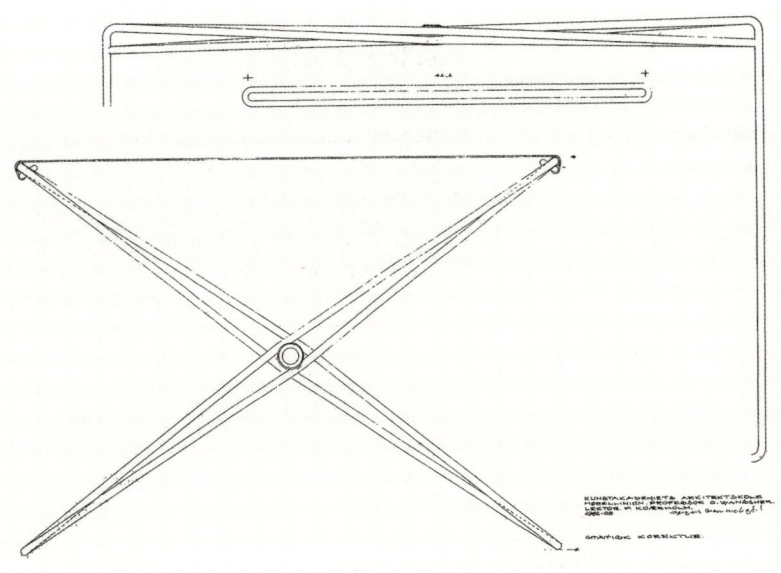

Working drawing by Jørgen Gammelgaard while he was a student at the Royal Danish Academy of Fine Arts, School of Architecture, the Furniture Line, in 1962–1963.

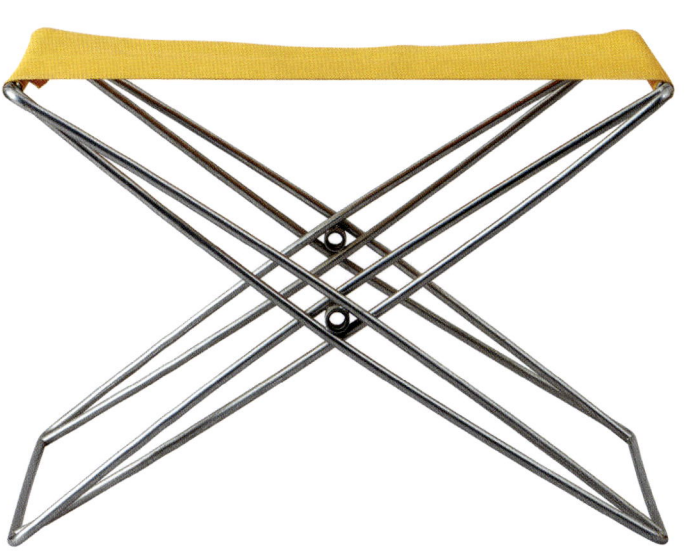

Propeller folding stool

Jørgen Gammelgaard
1938–1991

year: 1970
materials: Maple, rosewood, vellum, stainless steel
prod. by: Søren Risvang & Ernst Rasmussen
inv. no.: 407/2003

With his laminated maple and rosewood stool, Jørgen Gammelgaard surpassed his furniture professor predecessors in a different way than he did with the folding stool from 1963 (see page 28). The stool makes almost impossible demands on the cabinetmaker who twists the two propellers into shape. Despite its complexity (the many pieces of wood that are glued together), the finished stool, consisting of two propellers, is simpler than all the others, precisely because it consists of just two propellers.

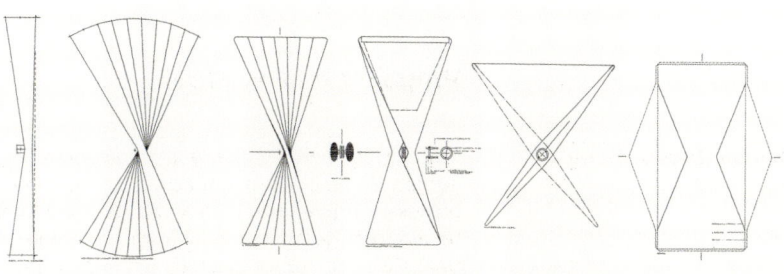

Drawing by Jørgen Gammelgaard
with descriptions, 1970.

Folding stool

Stig Herman Olsen
1949-

year: 1993
materials: Beech, textile
prod. by: Arne Kristensen
inv. no.: 152/2005

Stig Herman Olsen was also a student of Kjærholm's. His take on the folding stool was presented at the Cabinetmakers' Autumn Exhibition in 1993 and must be seen as an attempt to make the folding stool even simpler, without a joint to connect the two legs, which simply rest on top of one another. Thus, the stool can be completely flat when not in use.

Z-Down

Erik Magnussen
1940–2014

year: 1965
materials: Steel, canvas
prod. by: Torben Ørskov
inv. no.: 4/1970

Erik Magnussen's Z Chair is a folding stool with a backrest. But it is also a tubular-steel chair and a cantilever chair without back legs. The chair is extremely simple. There are no welded joints, just the joint between the two parts, where it folds. Magnussen's idea was to keep the stretched fabric (or leather) from going slack with time by having it constantly tightened by the frame. Despite its rigid appearance, the chair is springy and comfortable, as it gives slightly when you sit down. Consequently, it solves a number of problems that early tubular-steel designers had not addressed in the early decades of the 20th century.

Low easy chairs

The folding chair was a symbol of power, a royal seat, so when the German Ludwig Mies van der Rohe designed a chair for the Spanish royal couple to be presented at the 1929 Barcelona International Exposition, he turned to the X or scissor motif. The result was a light, low and open modernist chair. The folding motif has been revisited many times in history. Mies van der Rohe drew inspiration from folding stools on the Iberian Peninsula. In low easy chairs, the X folding motif was widely used during the early 20th century in connection with the furnishing of the large ocean liners, which in many ways became a source of inspiration for modernist architecture.

    In Denmark the low, open folding chair became popular due to the simplicity of its construction and the sleek body that lived up to the modernist call for honest and comprehensible construction and spatial transparency. Nothing should obstruct the gaze as it swept through the open spatial sequences of modernist architecture. The low chair allowed for a freer, less fixated seating position that harmonised with the more democratic spirit of the time. The low chair type was developed to include variants where the kinship with the folding chair was completely obscured.

38	The Barcelona Chair, Ludwig Mies van der Rohe
40	JH512, Hans J. Wegner
44	Prototype, Poul Kjærholm
48	EKC22, Poul Kjærholm
50	Eva, Bruno Mathsson
54	654W, Jens Risom

The Barcelona Chair

**Ludwig
Mies van der Rohe (DE)**
1886–1969

year:	1929
materials:	Chromed steel, leather
prod. by:	Knoll
inv. no.:	48/1977

Mies van der Rohe's Barcelona Chair was designed for the German pavilion at the 1929 Barcelona International Exposition, which the Spanish royal couple were going to visit. The chair draws inspiration both from the curule seat, the Roman official's seat, whose X-frame had always been a symbol of power and from the Greek *klismos* chair with its curved legs. With its open, geometric structure, the cubic space it outlines, the side arc and cool flat steel it became a symbol of the new modernist movement. It was to play a crucial role as a model for the many low modernist easy chairs that followed, especially in Denmark.

JH512

Hans J. Wegner
1914–2007

year:	1949
materials:	Oak, wicker
prod. by:	Johannes Hansen Møbelsnedkeri
inv. no.:	59/1950

Hans J. Wegner was the first Danish architect to introduce the low folding chair as an easy chair in the living room. The open or lightly padded chairs were a perfect fit for the open modernist architecture. Wegner was intrigued by the challenge of designing furniture for the cramped flats of the time. Thus, he saw it as an advantage that the chair could be folded and hung on the wall when not in use. JH512 was a striking example of how the folding chair, which Mies van der Rohe's Barcelona Chair (see page 39) had introduced to the modernist age, could be made human and tactile with oak and India cane without compromising on rationality. Every structural detail has an explanation, right down to the holes in the seat, which are not for decoration but occur because the cane strips cannot be wrapped around the part of the frame where the grips are attached.

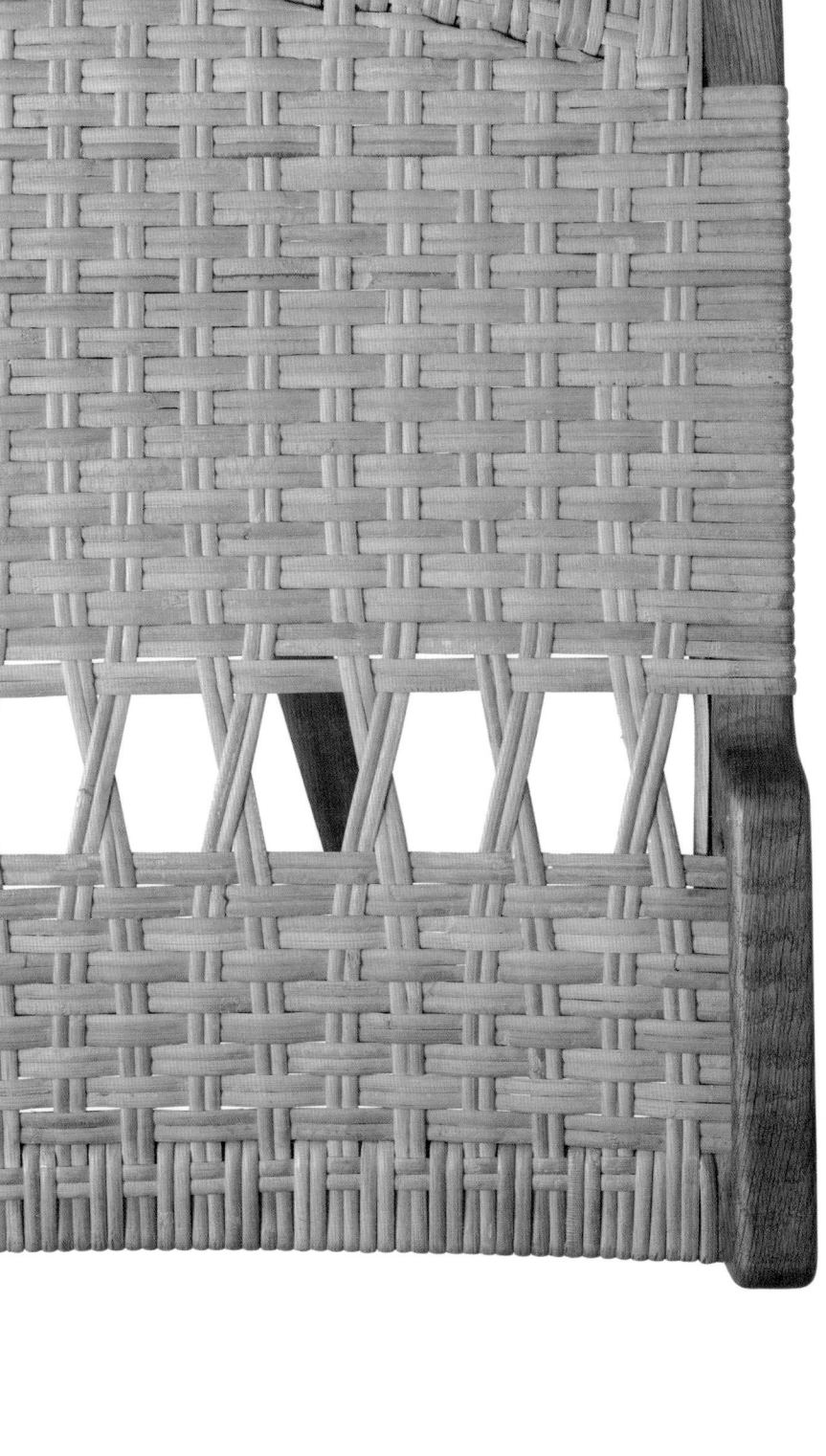

Low easy chairs | **JH512** – Hans J. Wegner

Cabinetmaker Johannes Hansen's stand at the Copenhagen Cabinetmakers' Guild's furniture exhibition in 1949 at Designmuseum Danmark. Hans J. Wegner's JH512 (see page 40) is seen in the background.

Low easy chairs | **JH512** — Hans J. Wegner

Prototype

Poul Kjærholm
1929–1980

year: 1951
materials: Chromed flat steel, flag halyard
inv. no.: 35/2011

This chair was Poul Kjærholm's graduation project at the School of Arts and Crafts. His supervisors were Hans J. Wegner and Bender Madsen. Kjærholm was clearly influenced by Wegner, who had reinterpreted Mies van der Rohe's Barcelona Chair in 1949 (JH512) (see page 40) and in 1950 had launched the Flag Halyard Chair. Kjærholm's idea of slitting the steel to make the arms and back had also occurred to Wegner in the context of a competition proposal for low-cost furniture design held by the Museum of Modern Art in New York in 1948.

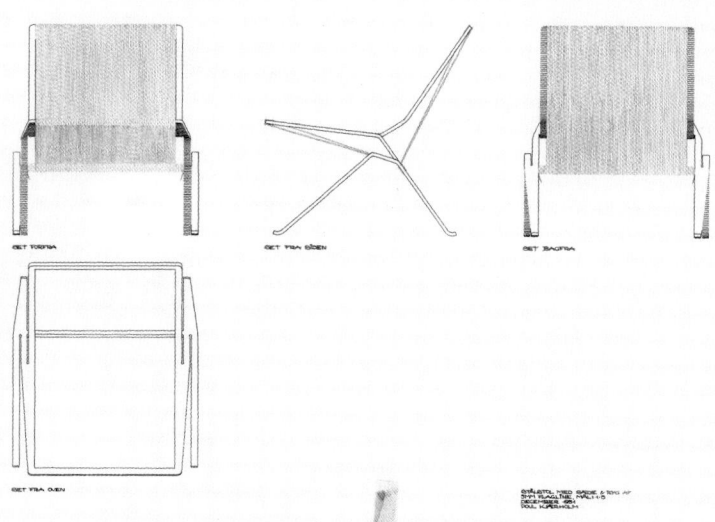

Poul Kjærholm's drawing for his graduation project at the Furniture School at the School of Arts and Crafts in 1951. The chair was later named PK25 (see page 45).

Poul Kjærholm's drawing of
EKC22, 1957 (see page 49).

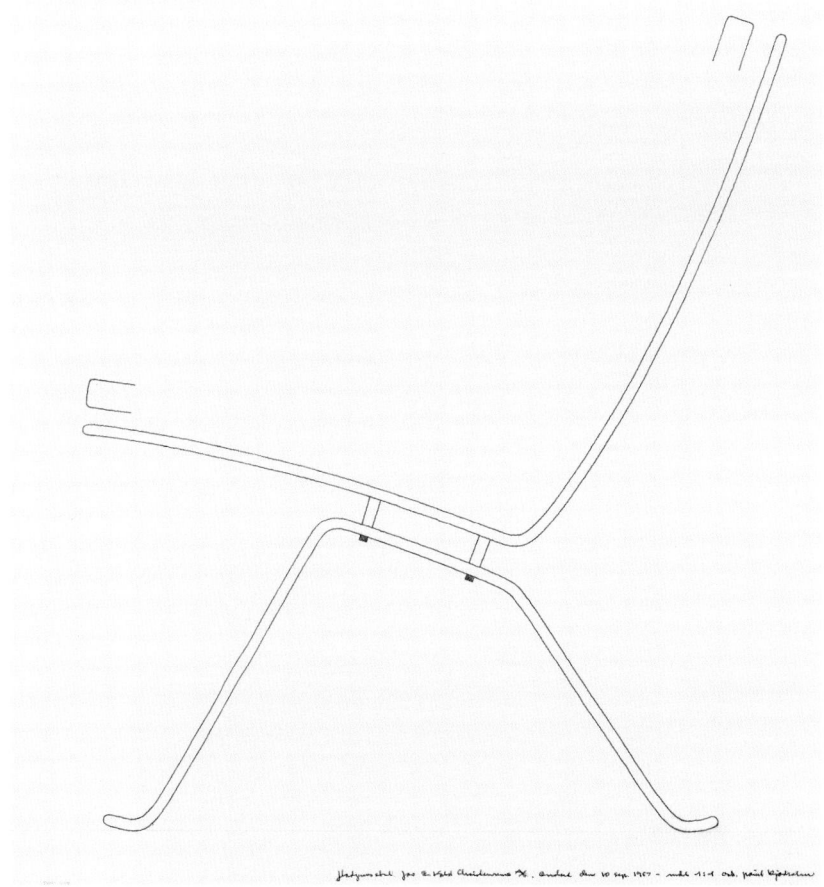

Low easy chairs | **EKC22** — Poul Kjærholm

EKC22

Poul Kjærholm
1929–1980

year:	1955–1957
materials:	Wicker, matt chromed steel
prod. by:	E. Kold Christensen
inv. no.:	116/1957

Kjærholm's EKC22 Chair was an elaboration of his graduation project (PK25) (see page 46). The chair is made of separate parts, which are not assembled with joints but rest loosely on top of one another, making it easy to decode the construction. EKC22 was the first chair for which Kjærholm used Allen screws. The chair was designed for low-cost flat-pack transport. Although Kjærholm was a trained cabinetmaker, for much of his life he strove to demonstrate that the right matt chromium plating could have the same sensual tactile qualities as natural materials. Thereby, he made the deliberately cool, industrial aesthetic of international modernism more human and Scandinavian.

Eva

Bruno Mathsson (SE)
1907–1988

year: 1933–1941
materials: Birch, webbing
prod. by: Karl Mathsson
inv. no.: 337/2004

Bruno Mathsson was a trained cabinetmaker and launched a production of laminated, steam-bent chairs at Värnamo in Sweden during the 1930s. Even though his steam-bent, laminated functionalist chairs resemble Alvar Aalto's from the same period, they have a much more luxurious look. Mathsson worked in much greater depth on adapting his chairs to the human body. The details are not strictly geometrical as in Aalto's furniture: for example, the tapered legs anticipate the organic modernism of the 1950s.

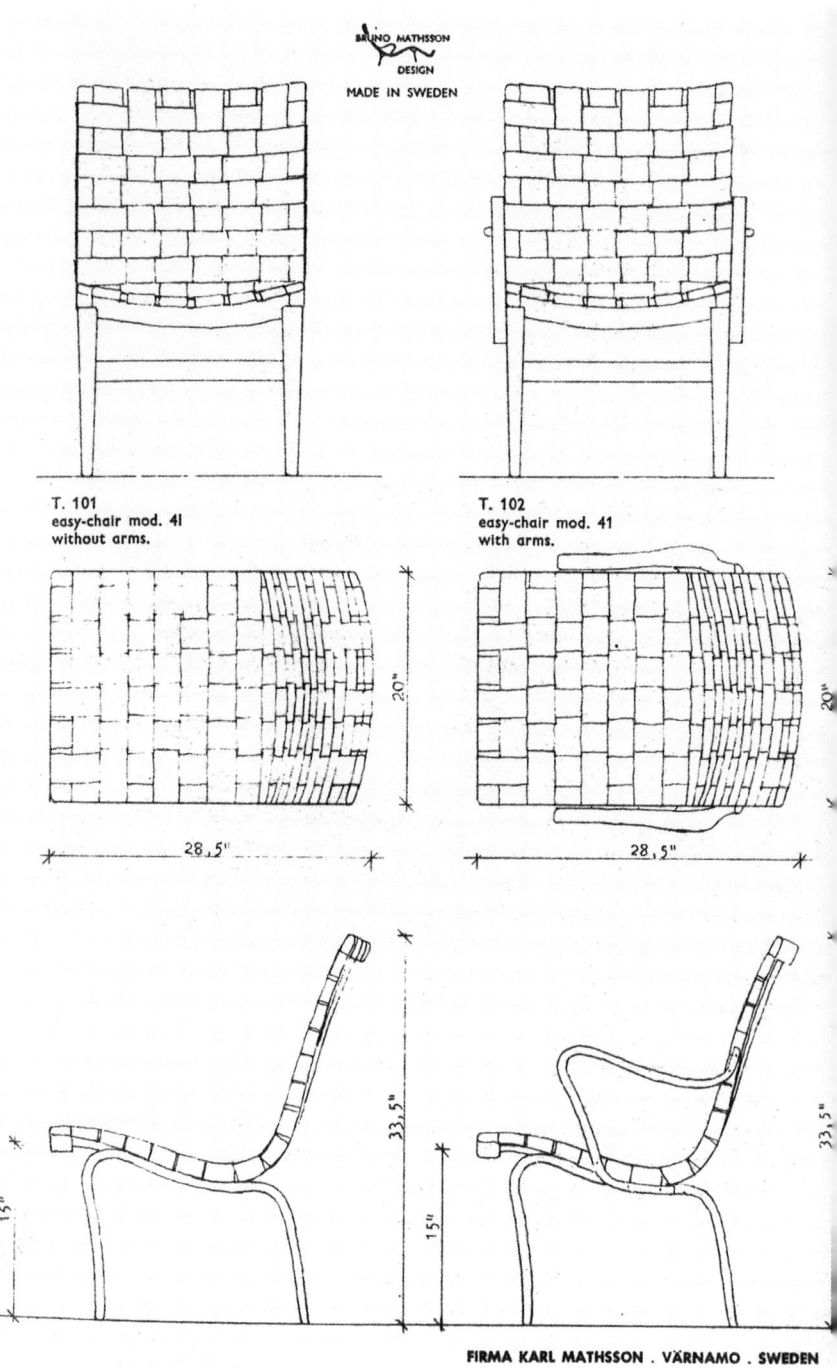

Bruno Mathsson, Eva, 1933–1944
(see page 50).

Jens Risom, 654W, 1941
(see page 55).

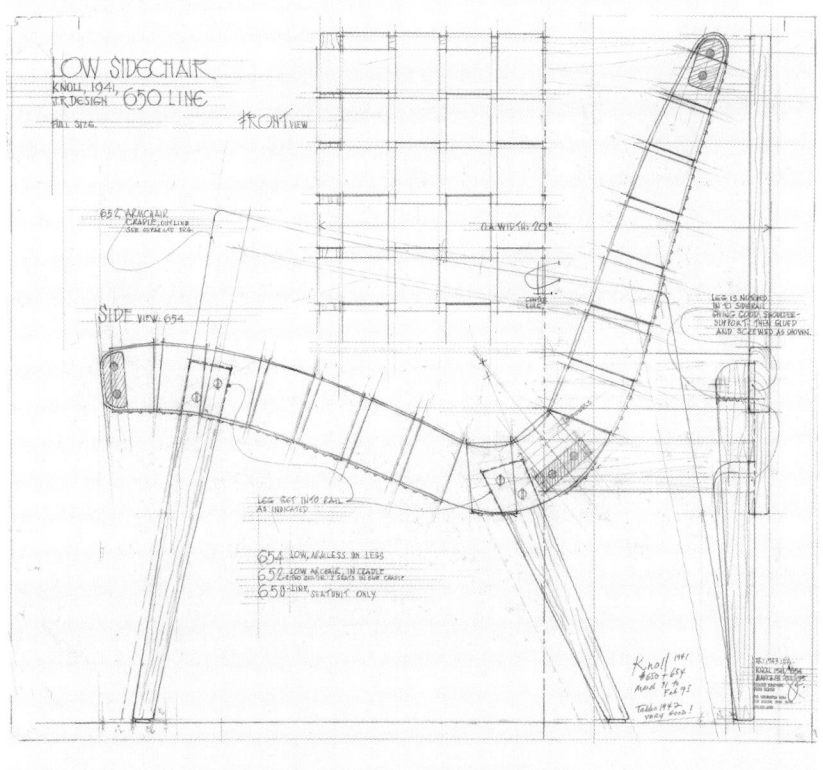

Low easy chairs | **654W** – Jens Risom

654W

Jens Risom
1916–2016

year:	1941
materials:	Birch, webbing
prod. by:	Knoll
inv. no.:	94/1997

Jens Risom trained as a furniture designer in Denmark at the School of Arts and Crafts and worked for a brief period in Stockholm, where he met Alvar Aalto and Bruno Mathsson, before making a name for himself as a major furniture designer in the United States. The first series Risom designed for Knoll (including 654W) was made during the early years of the war, when there was a scarcity of materials. Hence, he had to utilise remnants of webbing from the army. The chair's simple Scandinavian expression made it popular in the United States during the post-war years.

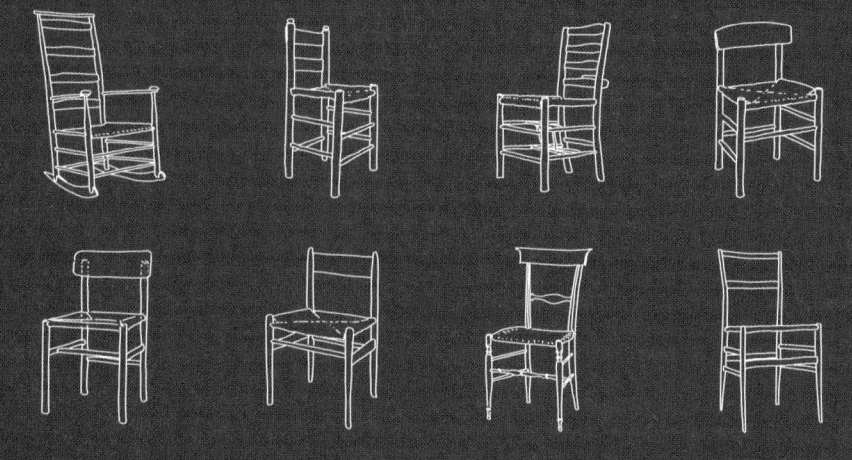

Peasant chairs

Denmark was an agricultural nation, so it was natural to base new chair designs on the simple rustic spindle-back type, although Danish designers turned mainly to Mediterranean peasant furniture for inspiration. The spindle-back type, which is still in use in the streets and bars throughout the Mediterranean region, has its origins in the Middle Ages. Instead of solid wood, the chair has a woven seat of rush, paper yarn or cane.

    The peasant chair with stretchers connecting the four corners was the inspiration for the furniture style of the 19th-century American Shaker sect, which also had influences from English neoclassicism. Shaker furniture was an important source of inspiration for the Danish modernists, who appreciated the austere pared-down look and slight dimensions of the moderate constructions. The furniture reflected the Christian sect's egalitarian and social community, which resembled the social, democratic society that was under development in Denmark during the 20th century. The call for affordable furniture with a rational and honest construction made peasant furniture an obvious choice in Denmark at a time when the country lacked advanced industrial production facilities.

58 —— Shaker rocking chair
60 —— Peasant chair
62 —— Church Chair, Kaare Klint
66 —— J39, The People's Chair, Børge Mogensen
68 —— Trattoria, Jasper Morrison
70 —— CH36, Hans J. Wegner
72 —— Campanino chair, Giovanni Battista di Ravenna
74 —— Superleggera, Gio Ponti

Shaker rocking chair

United States

year: 1850–1860
materials: Hickory, canvas webbing
inv. no.: A32/1935

The Shakers were an American sect whose members danced, clapped and shook during their religious services. The interiors of their homes were extremely austere: their furniture was a pared-down version of European spindle designs. The furniture was lightweight, unornamented and utilitarian. That is why it became a source of inspiration for many modernist furniture designers, particularly in Denmark.

Peasant chair

Southern Europe

year: 20th century
materials: Beech, seagrass
inv. no.: 138/2016

This peasant chair from Southern Europe was acquired for the Royal Danish Academy of Fine Arts, School of Architecture by Professor Kaj Gottlob. The history of the simple peasant chair dates back to the late Middle Ages, and in the early 20th century, many Danish architects embraced it as an honest, everyday chair that could be produced at an affordable price. It possessed the desired simple expression and transparent structure and did not require advanced production machinery. Designers often turned to the lighter, more refined versions, especially American Shaker furniture.

Church Chair

Kaare Klint
1888–1954

year: 1936
materials: Beech, Japanese seagrass
prod. by: Fritz Hansen
inv. no.: A33/1938

Kaare Klint took over the completion of his father's project, Grundtvig's Church in the north-west district of Copenhagen. For its tower, P. V. Jensen-Klint had purchased light peasant chairs. Inspired by these, Kaare Klint designed a more robust and comfortable version for the Bethlehem Church. He used steam-bent back posts and curved slats inspired by American Shaker furniture (see page 59). The frame is strongest in the middle, where the load is greatest. The Church Chair has a hymn-book shelf and room for a hat underneath the seat. Klint later designed a slightly larger version for Grundtvig's Church.

P. V. Jensen Klint, Grundtvig's Church.
The church was completed by his son,
Kaare Klint in 1940 (see page 63).

Peasant chairs | **Church Chair** – Kaare Klint

Børge Mogensen, J39, the People's Chair, 1947
(see page 67).

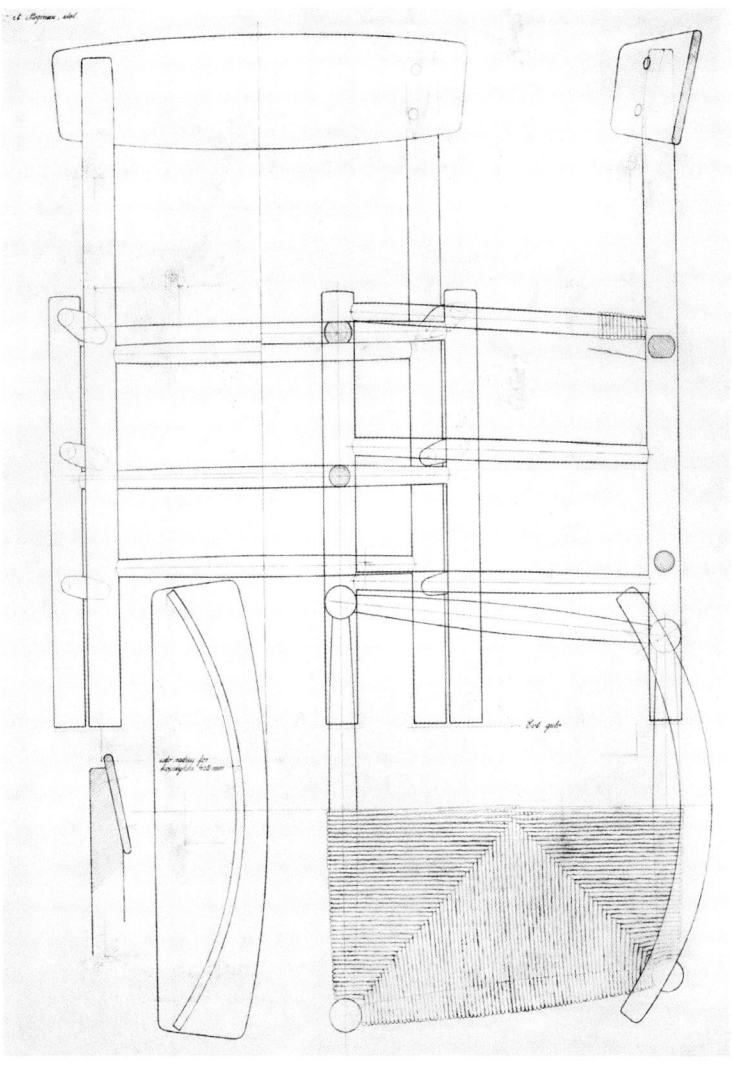

Peasant chairs | **J39, The People's Chair** – Børge Mogensen

J39, The People's Chair

Børge Mogensen
1914–1972

year: 1947
materials: Oak, paper yarn
prod. by: FDB Møbler
inv. no.: 20/1959

Børge Mogensen was a student of Kaare Klint's and his closest disciple. In 1942 he was appointed head of the furniture design studio of the Confederation of Danish Manufacturing and Retail Cooperatives (FDB), whose mission was to provide Danes with the highest-quality industrially produced furniture at the lowest possible price. He based the design on Kaare Klint's rustic Church Chair (see page 63), which he simplified, giving it straight back posts and a single curved back panel, which provides excellent lumbar support. The chair was both much cheaper and more comfortable. It was sometimes referred to as the Shaker Chair and was also a perfect match for the Shaker Table that Mogensen designed for FDB.

Trattoria

Jasper Morrison (UK)
1959-

year: 2009
materials: Beech, plastic
prod. by: Magis
inv. no.: 95/1911

The British designer Jasper Morrison is reminiscent of the mid-20th-century Danish designers in the way many of his designs draw on historical types. He strives to make his design 'super normal'. The inspiration from Børge Mogensen's People's Chair (J39) is obvious, but Morrison does not merely play with the look of the chair but also with our expectations, using plastic, a material that Mogensen did not consider suitable for furniture. He also picks up on the idea of the affordable popular chair with this knock-down construction that can be disassembled.

CH36

Hans J. Wegner
1914–2007

year:	1962
materials:	Oak, paper yarn
prod. by:	Carl Hansen & Søn
inv. no.:	71/2013

Hans J. Wegner's take on his friend Børge Mogensen's People's Chair was more Shaker-like in character. It was more slender and, like Shaker chairs, it had a back panel that was slotted into the back posts (see page 59). In a version with armrests (CH37), the front legs went up through the armrests as in a genuine Shaker chair. The legs were conical and thickest where they needed to support and be joined: in other words, at the seat. The rounded ends and conical legs were typical of Wegner and the style he represented: organic modernism. Consequently, the chair is perhaps much more a child of the Danish Modern aesthetic than Mogensen's Shaker Chair, which was more of a Danish people's chair.

Campanino chair

Giovanni Battista di Ravenna (IT)

year: ca. 1850
materials: Wood, wicker
prod. by: Lavagna
inv. no.: A12/1938

Giovanni Battista Ravenna's Campanino chair is a further development of the light, traditional shape, which had been produced in Chiavari in Italy since the early 19th century. Although the elegant chair has a touch of Empire style, it is also a slender refinement of the ancient peasant spindle chair. To some extent, this type of chair was outmatched when Thonet's bentwood chairs appeared in the second half of the 19th century. It was chairs like this that inspired Gio Ponti when he designed his Superleggera chair in the 1950s (see page 74).

Superleggera

Gio Ponti (IT)
1891–1979

year: 1957
materials: Hickory, cane
prod. by: Cassina
inv. no.: 49/1959

The Italian designer, Gio Ponti's legendary Superleggera (super lightweight) weighs only 1.7 kg and is basically a simplification of the classic spindle chair. Ponti based his design on the popular Chiavari chair (see page 72), which was a simple, cheap, lightweight chair dating from the early 19th century. Ponti reduced the number of spindles to a minimum, used strong ash or hickory and India cane. He made the spindles triangular and developed a special way of joining them that gave the chair its surprising strength. Ponti tested the chair by throwing it from the top of a four-storey building – it bounced up in the air like a ball, without shattering.

Peasant chairs | **Superleggera** – Gio Ponti (IT)

Ad for Gio Ponti's chair Superleggera from 1957 (see page 74).

Bentwood chairs

In the mid 19th century, the cabinetmaker Michael Thonet revolutionised furniture manufacturing in Austria with the first truly industrial chairs, made of a minimal number of components joined with bolts. The parts could be packed in boxes for ease of transport, like modern-day IKEA products. The steam-bending technology made it possible to reduce the number of parts and thus the costly joints. Central European modernists, such as Le Corbusier, found the chair exemplary, not only due to the low cost but also because of its simplicity and low weight. The Danish furniture designers also saw the potential of the type, the technology and the clean expression. The Thonet chair is essentially a modern simplification of peasant spindle-back chairs.

    The Danish furniture manufacturer Fritz Hansen mastered the steam bending of beech strips in the early 20th century. The company developed its own variants and produced bentwood furniture for the entire Scandinavian market during the 1930s. Some of the craft-oriented Danish designers were critical of the chair's uncontrolled forms and the lack of precision in steam bending. Still, the technology was used in several designs in combination with traditional cabinetmaker's techniques during the 20th century, and by the 1970s manufacturers had achieved a higher degree of control over the shape of the bent wood thanks to a new technology: precompression, where the wood is put under pressure during the heating process, which makes it more supple and bendable.

80	Chair for Søndermark Chapel, Frits Schlegel
84	No. 14, Michael Thonet
86	DAN chair, Søren Hansen
90	No. 209, Thonet Design Team
94	EKC12, Poul Kjærholm
96	PK15, Poul Kjærholm
100	FH9230, Henning Larsen
102	Moku, Cecilie Manz

Chair for Søndermark Chapel, Copenhagen

Frits Schlegel
1896–1965

year: 1927–1930
materials: Beech, webbing
prod. by: Fritz Hansen
inv. no.: 197/2005

The back of Frits Schlegel's chair for Søndermark Chapel is bentwood, and so are the spindles in the backrest. The advantage of steam bending is that it eliminates the need for joints. This makes production cheaper and creates a different aesthetic from that of a traditional spindle chair. However, the undercarriage of this chair is constructed with rungs like a traditional peasant spindle chair. Thus, the chair comes across as a synthesis of the ancient peasant chair and the bentwood Vienna chair.

Fritz Schlegel's chairs in
Søndermark Chapel (see page 81).

Transport case with
Thonet Chair No. 14
(see page 84).

Bentwood chairs | **No. 14** — Michael Thonet

No. 14

Michael Thonet (AT)

year: 1859
materials: Beech, wickerwork
prod. by: Gebrüder Thonet
inv. no.: 22d/1970

Michael Thonet's Chair No. 14 is considered to be the first industrial chair. By steam bending beech wood Thonet succeeded in revolutionising furniture manufacture, avoiding expensive carpentry joints and reducing the design to a few elements that were assembled with bolts. The chairs were cheap to transport, because they could be packed flat. Thirty-six chairs took up only one cubic metre of space during transport. In the 20th century, this simple, lightweight chair became a model for the modernist movement, even though by then it was an old chair.

DAN Chair

Søren Hansen
1905–1977

year: 1930
materials: Beech
prod. by: Fritz Hansen
inv. no.: 83/1987

Fritz Hansen produced bentwood chairs identical to Thonet's Vienna chairs, and from the late 1920s in extremely large quantities. However, the DAN Chair was the factory's own design. The present version was designed by the managing director, Søren Hansen, who was third generation in the company. The round seat of the bentwood Vienna chair has been replaced by a seat with a freely shaped contour and the back bracket is without reinforcements. It is low and more curved, thus adapting to the shape of the sitter's lower back. However, this minimalist take on a Vienna chair is not particularly comfortable.

Production of the DAN Chair at FritzHansen, 1930s (see page 87).

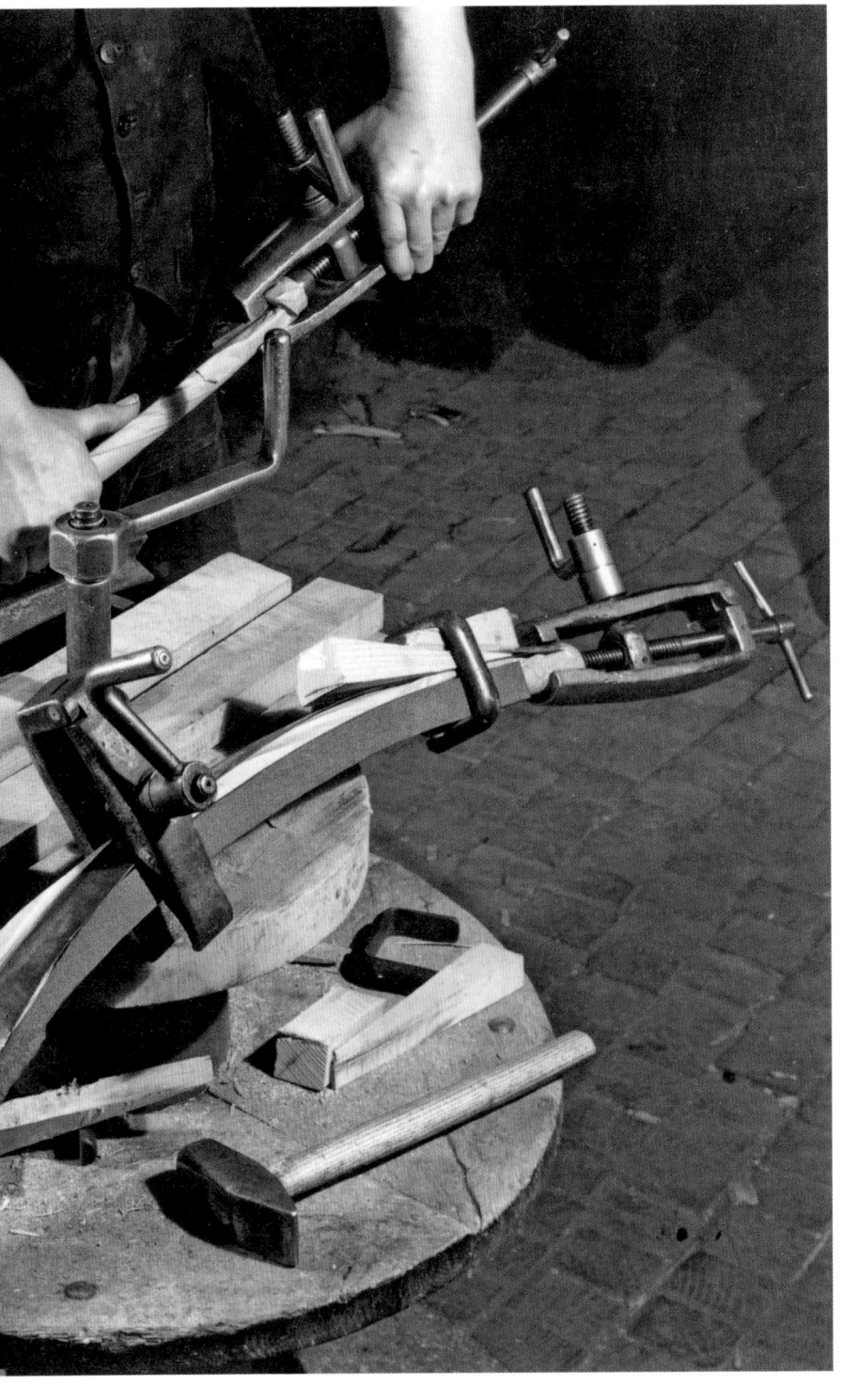

No. 209

Thonet Design Team (AT)

year: 1900
materials: Beech, cane
prod. by: Gebrüder Thonet
inv. no.: 261a-b/1990

Using steam-bending technology, Thonet revolutionised furniture making. It became industrial. This iconic type is a refinement of the ancient frame chair. Steam bending did away with many expensive joints, and the chairs could be shipped disassembled. In the 1920s, Poul Henningsen was photographed with the chair balanced on his index finger, praising it to the skies because it was lightweight, cheap and solved its social task. Professor of Furniture Ole Wanscher disagreed. He thought the steam-bent structures led to a significant waste of material. What was cut away could just as well have been used for traditional joints, which were less restrictive for the shape than the clumsy way the bentwood chair was bolted together.

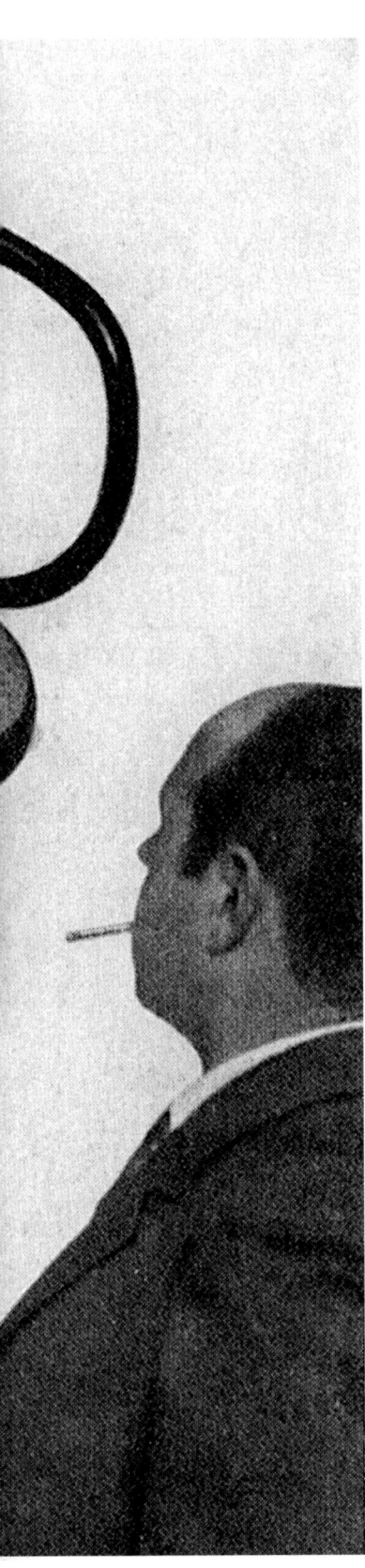

The architect, designer and social critic Poul Henningsen with Thonet Chair No. 209 (see page 90) in the magazine *Kritisk Revy* (Critical Revue), December 1927.

EKC12

Poul Kjærholm
1929–1980

year:	1962
materials:	Steel, leather
prod. by:	E. Kold Christensen
inv. no.:	534/2008

With this chair Kjærholm sought to surpass several of the Bauhaus architects' tubular-steel furniture in simplicity. The chair comprises two bent tubes and a seat. Actually, its shape is taken from the old bentwood chair, Thonet No. 209. As an elegant feature, the two bent poles do not touch at the top rail (the back). The chair comes across simultaneously as a classic frame chair and, by virtue of its material, as an international modern chair.

PK15

Poul Kjærholm
1929–1980

year:	1979
materials:	Ash, wickerwork
prod. by:	PP Møbler
inv. no.:	74/1984

Kjærholm's tubular-steel chair is much heavier than it looks (se page 94). This chair is as light as a classical bentwood chair. The precise, clear-cut shape that Kjærholm sought is not possible in steam bending; that is precisely the reason why the bentwood chairs are more curved. However, the new precompression technology, where the wood is put under pressure in a longitudinal direction while wet, made it possible. The procedure folds the wood's cells transversely, so the wood can be bent. For the structure to hold, Kjærholm had to incorporate a connecting piece between the two back rails and an extra ring under the seat for reinforcement.

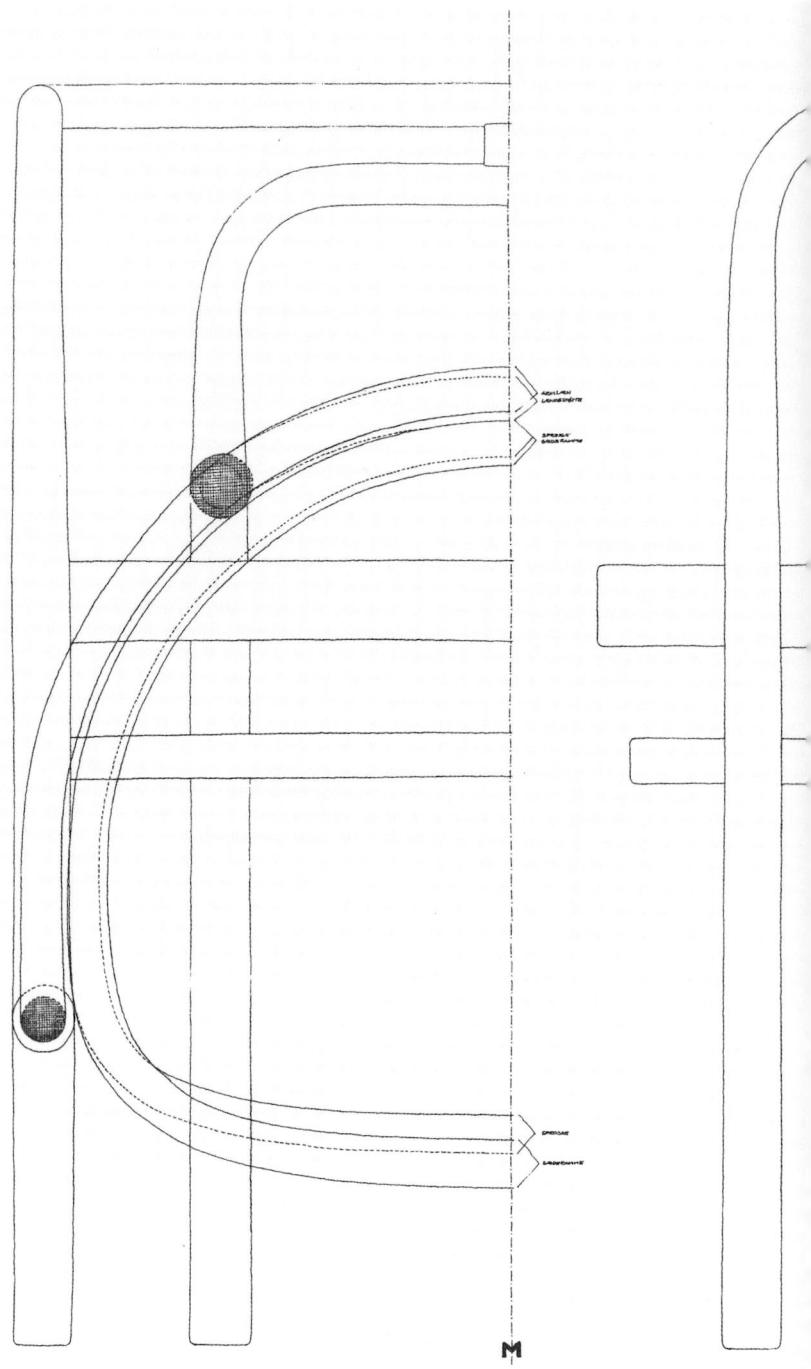

Poul Kjærholm, PK15, 1979 (see page 97).

99

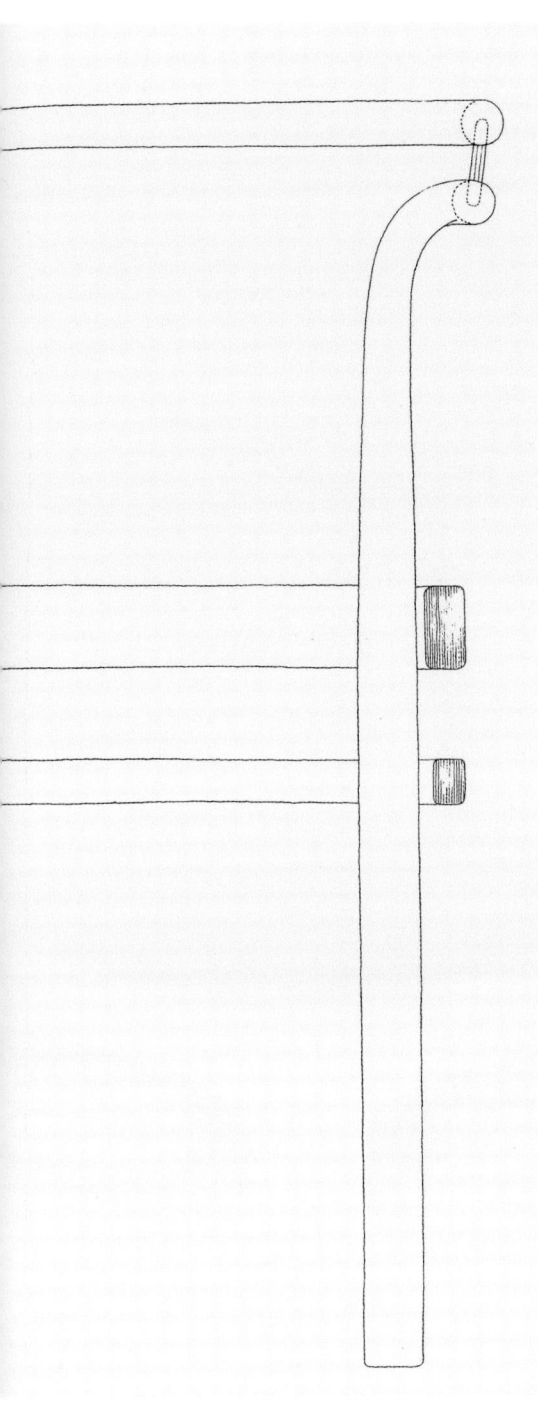

FH9230

Henning Larsen
1925–2013

year: 1967
materials: Aluminium, chromed steel tube, leather
prod. by: Fritz Hansen
inv. no.: 123/1985

Henning Larsen's Café Chair is based on the motif of Kjærholm's tubular-steel frame chair (see page 94). However, Larsen makes steel braces out of the front and back legs. This achieves a vertical gap in the back, which may seem to allow space for the spine. However, the chair is proportioned like a proper café chair: a chair one cannot sit in for very long, as it is not particularly ergonomic.

Moku

Cecilie Manz
1972-

year:	2016
materials:	Japanese beech
prod. by:	Actus / Nissin Mokkou
inv. no.:	137/2016

Like Denmark, Japan has a highly sophisticated craft culture, and Danish design is highly prized in Japan, which, also like Denmark, cultivates simplicity, detail and tactility. The distinguished Actus/Nissin cabinetmaker's workshop contacted the Danish designer Cecilie Manz because they wanted a chair with Scandinavian features designed for the Japanese market. The light chair combines characteristics from the Danish tradition of steam-bent chairs and from the bentwood chairs. It is made of steam-bent Japanese beech, and the seat is slightly reminiscent of Fritz Hansen's Dan Chair from the 1920s. However, the expression is sharper and cleaner. The straight sides of the frame and the extra slat in the back make the chair comfortable, and it is low enough to push under a dining table. The chair is an excellent example of how Danish modernism and the related frame-chair tradition are still alive and evolving, even in other countries.

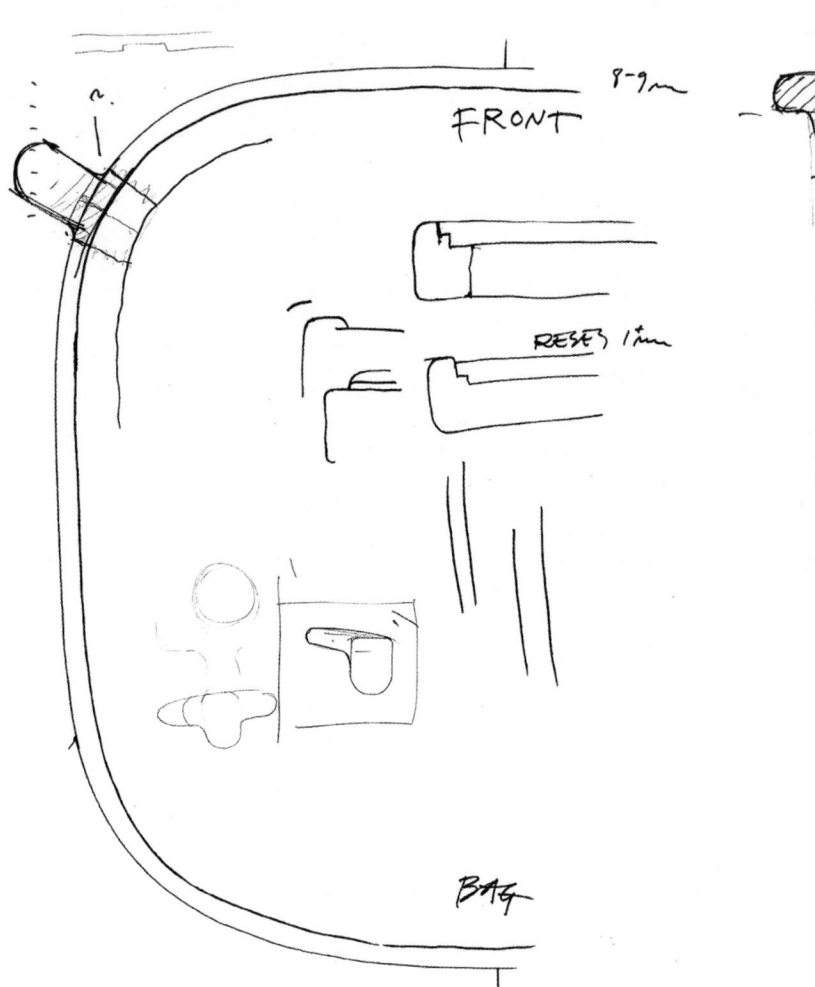

Cecilie Manz, Moku, 2016
(see page 102).

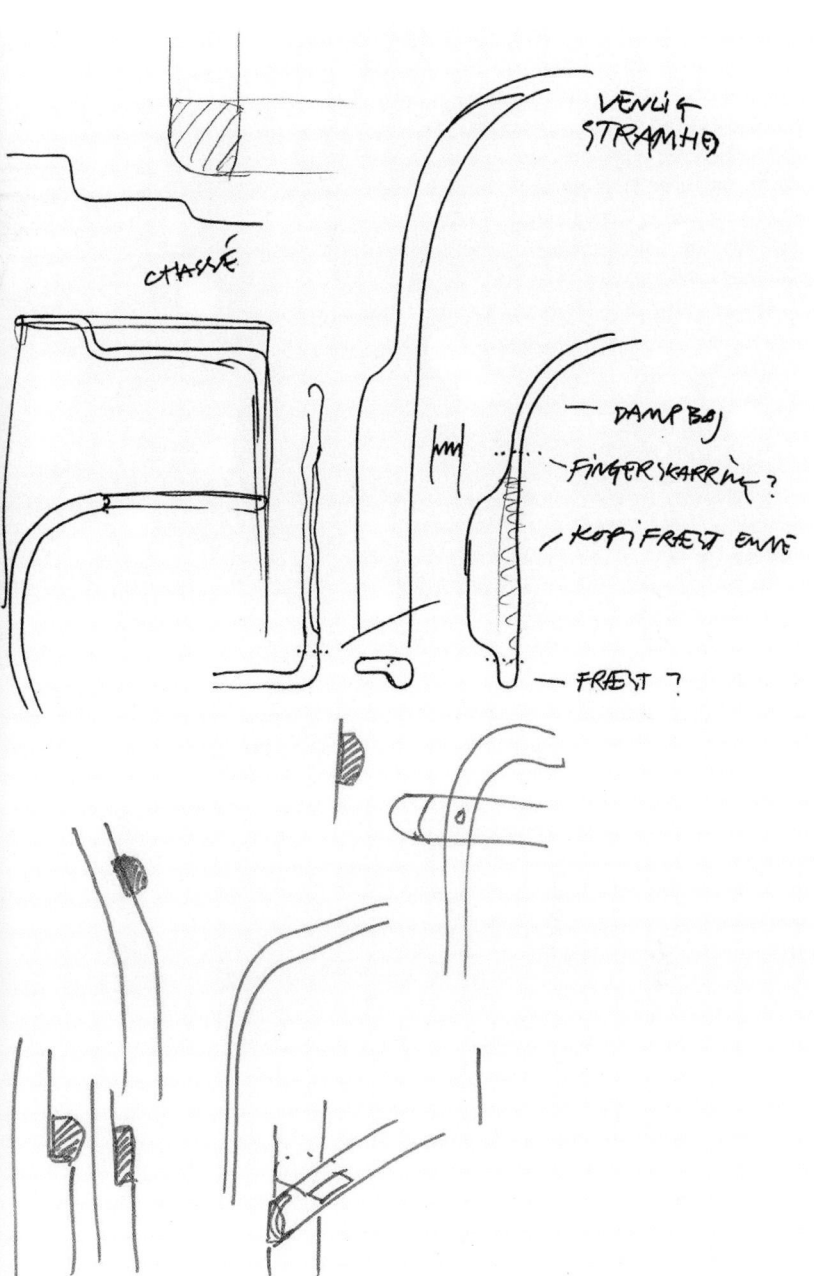

Chinese chairs

Chinese furniture, especially cane furniture, had been popular in Europe for centuries, while the interest in the wooden chair with the curvy splat emerged during the modernist era. Professor Kaare Klint and his students worked on Chinese details, either taken directly from Chinese models or via English furniture design. Klint's student and successor as professor, Ole Wanscher, wrote in his 1932 book Møbeltyper:

'Overall, the stylistic expression of Chinese chairs is conditioned by the at once naive and sophisticated combination of details, which may be either naturally constructive or merely decorative elements.'

It was the simple, honest construction of the chairs that held the interest of the functionalists, not their function as ceremonial thrones. Ole Wanscher, Hans J. Wegner and Finn Juhl, among others, were inspired by the curvature of the splats and arms – they refined these elements and incorporated them into the organic modernism in Danish furniture design.

108	Chinese chair
110	The Bone Chair, Finn Juhl
114	FH1783, Hans J. Wegner
116	The Wishbone Chair, Hans J. Wegner
120	Bac, Jasper Morrison
122	Chinese chair
124	Chair for the Bellevue Theatre restaurant, Arne Jacobsen
128	The Valet Chair, Hans J. Wegner

Chinese chair

China

year: ca. 1800
materials: Chinese rosewood, huang hua li
inv. no.: 265/1989

A chair of this type is illustrated in Ole Wanscher's 1932 book, Møbeltyper (Furniture Types). It was this illustration that inspired Wegner and other of his contemporaries to take up the type. One of the aspects that fascinated the modernists was the contrast between a heavy, static, square base and a light, dynamic upper part: geometrical versus organic. As early as the 18th century, the Chinese chairs had taught Europeans that it is the upper part of the chair that gives a designer scope to vary the chair's expression and invest it with life. Even though the chair's concave backrest continues out to the sides, it does not form armrests as on a modern chair. The function of the upper part was to create a beautiful frame around the seated person.

The Bone Chair

Finn Juhl
1912–1989

year: 1944
materials: Cuban mahogany, leather
prod. by: Niels Vodder
inv. no.: 4/1992

As the name suggests, Finn Juhl's Bone Chair is organic or, in Juhl's own words, 'animalistically satisfying'. The parts flow imperceptibly into one other, the joints are concealed in the shape, and the material is at its thickest where it is subject to the greatest impact. In this respect, the Bone Chair was inspired by ancient Chinese chairs, as were the bulges of the armrests. Wegner was influenced by this chair when he designed his Round Chair (see page 160), which, without crossbars and with more flowing lines, comes across as a simplification of Juhl's chair.

Cabinetmaker Niels Vodder's stand at the Copenhagen Cabinetmakers' Guild's furniture exhibition, 1944, featuring Finn Juhl's Bone Chair, NV44, (see page 111).

Chinese chairs | **The Bone Chair** – Finn Juhl

Exhibition stand for Fritz Hansen with furniture by Hans J. Wegner. The chair is FH1783, 1945 (see page 114).

Chinese chairs | **FH1783** – Hans J. Wegner

FH1783

Hans J. Wegner
1914–2007

year: 1945
materials: Ash, paper yarn
prod. by: Fritz Hansen
inv. no.: 160/1989

Fritz Hansen manufactured bentwood furniture, Vienna chairs, but during the war the company ran into problems with sourcing long pieces of beech wood. Wegner was asked whether he could design a chair with shorter pieces of steam-bent beech wood. Between 1944 and 1945, Wegner designed four variants, based on a photo of an ancient Chinese chair. He felt that the lastest one (from 1945) was the most accomplished. The refined Chinese chair had become a Danish popular chair with a peasant-style undercarriage. It is purged of ornamentation and consists of regular rounded poles. Nevertheless, it is still monumental and 'majestic': not the 'quick', lightweight bentwood chair that Fritz Hansen had requested.

Chinese chairs | **FH1783** – Hans J. Wegner

The Wishbone Chair

Hans J. Wegner
1914–2007

year: 1950
materials: Ash, paper yarn
prod. by: Carl Hansen & Søn
inv. no.: 217/1987

After Wegner had gained international success with The Chair (see page 160), he was asked whether he could design a chair that had the same qualities that was cheaper to manufacture. The result was the Wishbone Chair, which was to become Wegner's most successful chair. The Wishbone Chair was Wegner's take on a modern, bentwood chair. The reason for its success may be its graphic, expressive appearance, or maybe the fact that anyone can recognise an archetype in it. It is a frame chair like the ancient *klismos* chairs (see page 135). It has a steam-bent backrest and a Chinese splat (see page 108), and the fragmentation of the backrest is reminiscent of the slanted struts on Windsor chairs (see page 204), while the undercarriage has similarities with old peasant chairs (see page 60). Wegner's Wishbone Chair is not only a refinement of a traditional type, it is also a synthesis of several different models and hence something completely new.

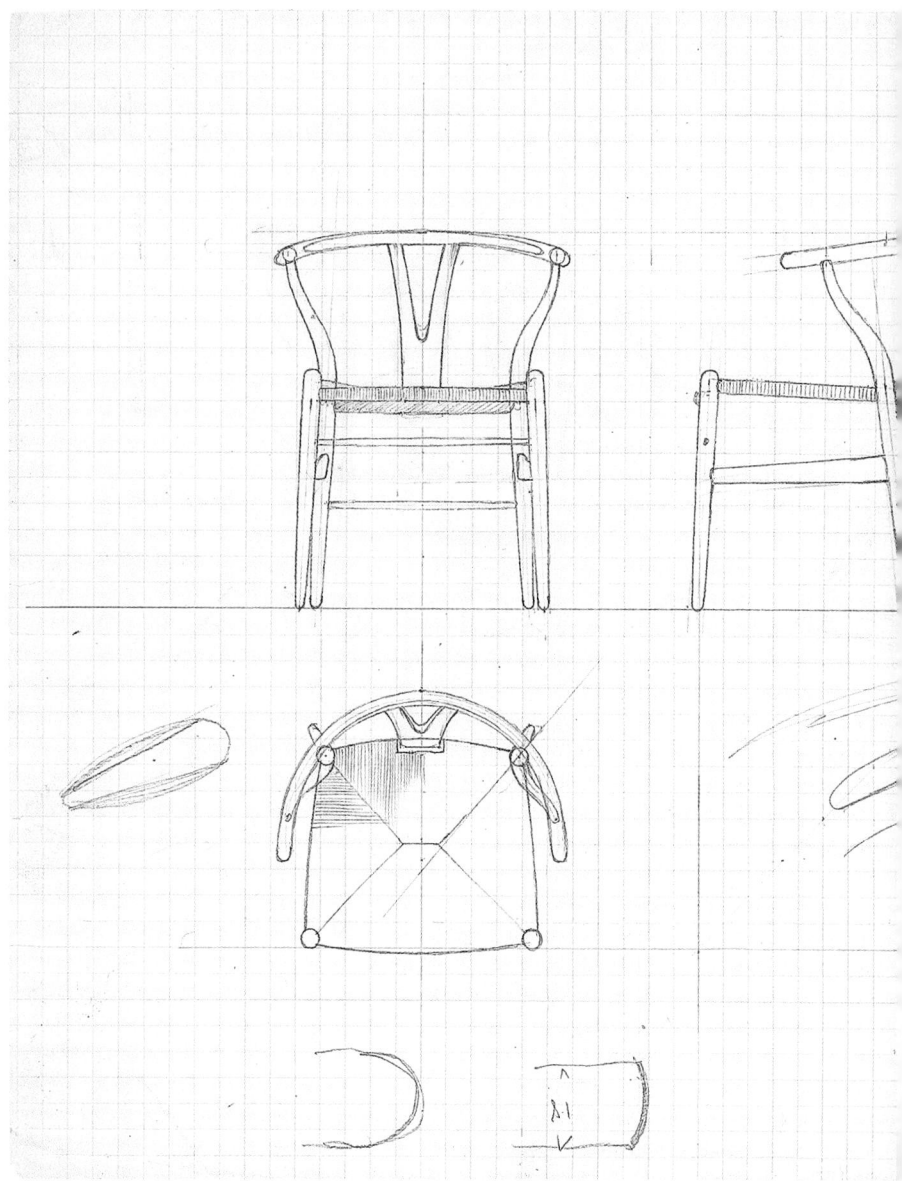

Hans J. Wegner, drawing of the Wishbone Chair, 1950 (see page 117).

Stol med rund Ryg 1:10
Hans J. Wegner.

Bac

Jasper Morrison (UK)
1959-

year: 2009
materials: Ash, plywood
prod. by: Cappellini
inv. no.: 59/2014

Like many Danish designers, when he designs something new, the British designer Jasper Morrison bases his work on traditional quality chair types. Bac is the result of Morrison's study of Wegner's Wishbone Chair (see page 117), among others. Morrison's Bac is a synthesis of previous types of furniture, just as much of Wegner's furniture was. With its slanted back, it calls to mind Wegner's chairs and Chinese chairs, while its moulded plywood shell seat is reminiscent of Arne Jacobsen's Series 7 Chair (see page 254). In other words, in this chair Morrison combined the two most popular Danish chairs of the 20th century.

Chinese chair

China

year: ca. 1800
materials: Padouk wood, straw
inv. no.: B27/1938

Designmuseum Danmark acquired the Chinese 'pendant lamp chair' in 1938 as an example of a knock-down construction. It could be dismantled easily, and Orla Mølgaard-Nielsen, the head of the Furniture School, which was located at Designmuseum Danmark, realised the potential: disassembled furniture is cheap to transport. A number of the school's students analysed the chair, among them were Hans J. Wegner and Børge Mogensen. The chair is characterised by the contrast between the geometrically rigorous base and the more organic curvature of the upper section. The flowing lines of the upper section inspired the evolution of the organic idiom embraced by Hans J. Wegner, among others.

Chair for the Bellevue Theatre restaurant

Arne Jacobsen
1902–1971

year: 1934
materials: Beech, oxhide
prod. by: Fritz Hansen
inv. no.: 180/1993

For the white, cubist development of Bellevue, north of Copenhagen, that Arne Jacobsen designed, he was also commissioned to design the interior of a restaurant. The chair for the restaurant was steam-bent at Fritz Hansen, a leading manufacturer of bentwood furniture. The seat resembles that of German tubular-steel furniture of the time, which appeared in cubist architecture with stretched leather and no padding. However, Jacobsen's chair is not only forward-looking, it also has a Chinese backrest, which makes it the first modern, Chinese-influenced chair. It is an idiosyncratic synthesis of many elements, some square, others round.

Arne Jacobsen, Bellevue Theatre
restaurant. The chair (see page 125)
was designed for the restaurant in 1934.

Chinese chairs | **Chair for the Bellevue Theatre restaurant** – Arne Jacobsen

The Valet Chair

Hans J. Wegner
1914–2007

year: 1953
materials: Teak, oak, brass
prod. by: Johannes Hansen Møbelsnedkeri
inv. no.: 106/1985

The Valet Chair came about because Wegner was commissioned to design clothes racks for a hotel. Initially, in 1951, he designed a four-legged version, which King Frederik IX wanted to buy. However, Wegner was not satisfied. His previous work with three-legged chairs and Chinese splats provided the inspiration for perhaps the most organic and, in terms of craftsmanship, most demanding chair in the Danish Modern movement. The user can hang his suit jacket on the backrest and place his wallet and keys in a small space inside the seat, which can be folded up to hold a pair of pressed trousers. The chair clearly mimics the human body with shoulders, spine and posterior. The S-shaped backrest is part of the actual structure rather than an inserted element as in the Chinese chairs.

Hans J. Wegner, the Valet Chair, 1953
(see page 128).

Chinese chairs | **The Valet Chair** — Hans J. Wegner

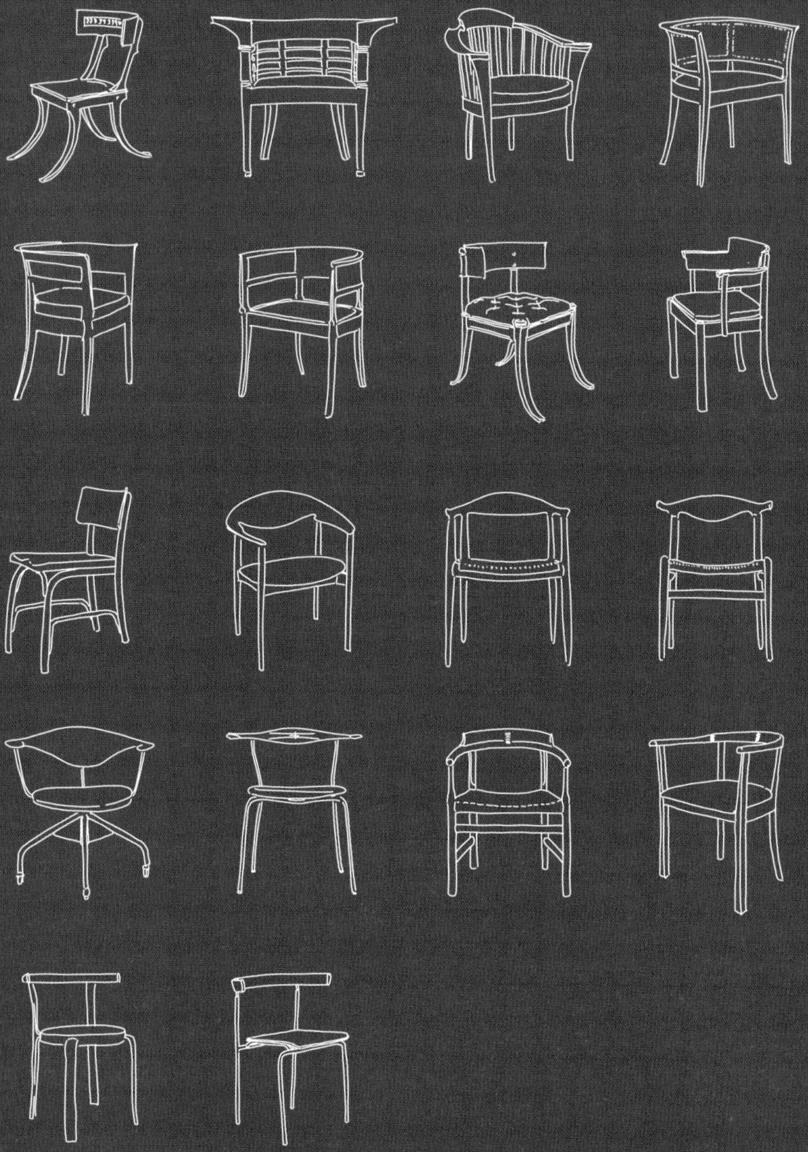

Frame chairs

Frame chairs occupy a key place in the history of Danish furniture design. It is a type that most Danish furniture designers have tried their hand at over the past 200 years. Although the type has been common in many countries, Danish stands out by having a dedicated name for it – *karmstol*, literally frame chair: a chair where the extended top rail offers support for the elbows and often continues to and rests on the front legs.

The type has its origins in the ancient Greek *klismos* chair, which was recreated by Danish Golden Age painters during the first half of the 19th century for use in their homes. It is a monumental piece of furniture, where the splat frames and presents the sitter, but also a simple solution, where the armrest is integrated into the backrest. Properly designed, the chair offers good lumbar support. The type is also known throughout Central Europe. The Smoker's or Captain's chair, which is a Windsor chair, belongs to same family, its lineage stretching back to antiquity. In Denmark, the type is part of the interest in neoclassicism in Danish design that has lasted since the 18th century until today, to varying degrees.

134	*Klismos* chair, N. A. Abildgaard
136	Chair for Dr Alfred Pers, Johan Rohde
138	Frame chair, P. V. Jensen Klint
140	The Faaborg Chair, Kaare Klint & Carl Petersen
144	Frame chair for Dansk Kunsthandel, Kaare Klint
148	Frame chair for Thorvaldsens Museum, Kaare Klint
150	*Klismos* chair, Kaj Gottlob
152	Frame chair, Edvard Thomsen
154	School chair, Frits Schlegel
156	The Metropolitan Chair, Aksel Bender Madsen & Ejner Larsen
160	The Chair, Hans J. Wegner
162	The Cow Horn Chair, Hans J. Wegner
164	Swivel chair, Hans J. Wegner
166	JH701, Hans J. Wegner
168	PP63, Hans J. Wegner
170	Frame chair, Ole Wanscher
172	8002, Chair for Café Victor, Rud Thygesen & Johnny Sørensen
174	Chair no. 10, Skagen, Jørgen Gammelgaard

Klismos chair

N. A. Abildgaard
1743–1809

year: 1790–1792
materials: Gold-plated beech
inv. no.: 1336

The Danish Golden Age painters (ca. 1800–50), who travelled to Italy and Greece, had a profound interest in antiquity. Several of them commissioned furniture, which they knew from antique vases and commemorative stelae.
N. A. Abildgaard was the first furniture designer to tackle the *klismos* chair (commonly known as 'the philosopher's chair') with its curved legs and large, concave backrest, which encloses the seated person. Over time, the type evolved into a Danish frame chair. Most Danish furniture designers have tried their hand at this type of chair, which is characterised by the concave backrest that becomes the armrests. The clarity and simplicity of antiquity was revisited over and over again in Danish furniture history; initially in the form of neoclassicism and later in modernism and minimalism.

Chair for Dr Alfred Pers

Johan Rohde
1856–1935

year:	1898
materials:	Mahogany, leather, brass
prod. by:	Brødrene H.P. & L. Larsen
inv. no.:	95/2012

Johan Rohde designed this chair for Dr Alfred Pers, the chief surgeon at Frederiks Hospital, which now houses Designmuseum Danmark. Although Rohde was a painter, he also had a keen interest in furniture design. He was one of the first advocates of simple furniture. He was inspired by both the shapes of antiquity and Japonism, but in many respects he anticipated Danish modernist furniture design. He taught Kaare Klint, when the latter was studying painting, and encouraged Klint's progression into the furniture field. This expressive frame chair anticipates Kaare Klint and Carl Petersen's Faaborg Chair, which is considered one of the purest Danish frame chairs.

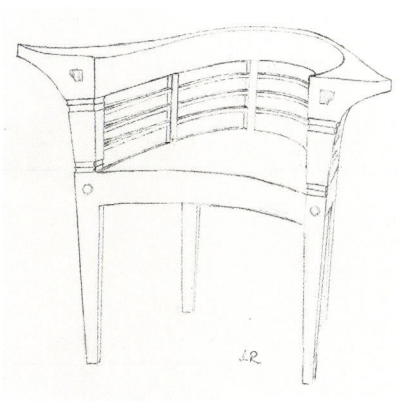

Johan Rohde, drawing of the chair for Dr Alfred Pers, ca. 1898.

Frame chair

P. V. Jensen Klint
1853–1930

year: ca. 1910
materials: Cuban mahogany, leather
inv. no.: 312/2004

The architect P. V. Jensen Klint, Kaare Klint's father, designed furniture in an eclectic, expressive idiom. This frame chair also references to antiquity with the volutes on top of the armrests, but does not otherwise cultivate the classicism that is a feature of his son, Kaare Klint's frame-chair designs. P. V. Jensen Klint's frame chair should probably be seen more in the context of peasant chairs with rounded backrests or the Smoker's and Captain's Chairs in the Windsor-chair tradition: chairs with a rounded backrest and an upright spindle or slat back.

The Faaborg Chair

Kaare Klint
1888–1954
—
Carl Petersen
1874–1923

year: 1914
materials: Oak burl, wickerwork
prod. by: N.M. Rasmussen
inv. no.: 26/1960

Klint and Petersen's chair for the Faaborg Museum is not a Klismos chair (see page 135) but reintroduces neoclassicism to Danish furniture design, turning it into the chair that is regarded as the very epitome of a Danish frame chair: a chair, to which many later Danish designers relate. This type of chair with a backrest that turns into armrests, embracing and framing the seated person, is also seen in many other countries. It was particularly prevalent in the avant-garde environment that surrounded the Wiener Werkstätte in Vienna around 1900. Barrel-shaped furniture is also familiar from the Windsor tradition and from designers such as Charles Rennie Mackintosh in Scotland, Richard Riemerschmid and Henry van de Velde in Germany and Frank Lloyd Wright in the United States. In fact, this type of chair already existed in Denmark in the early 20th century. Fritz Hansen produced a chair very similar to the Faaborg Chair. The Faaborg Chair's light, strict, geometric shape was specifically designed for the galleries where it would be used.

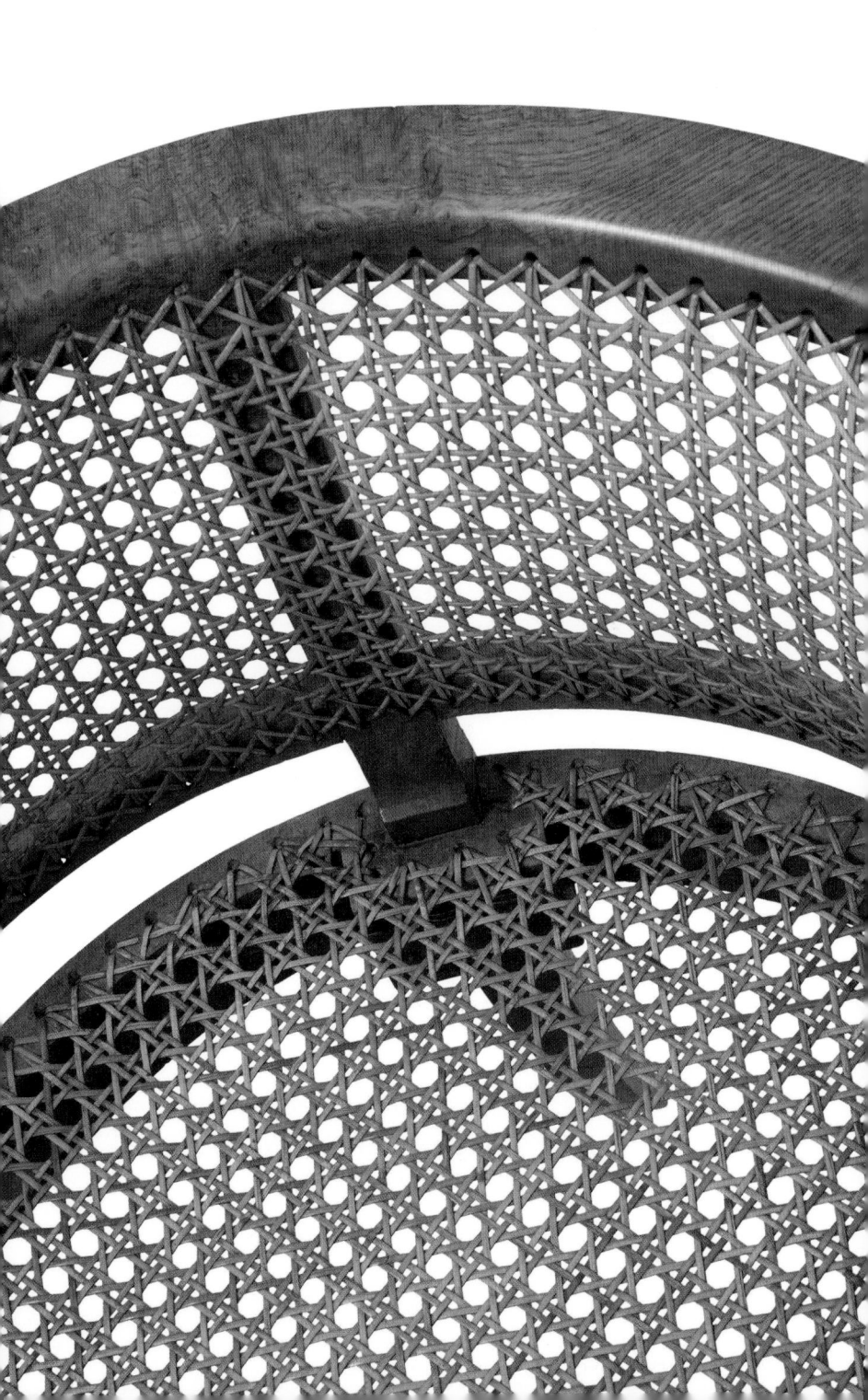

Kaare Klint and Carl Petersen, the Faaborg Chair (see page 140) in the painting gallery at Faaborg Museum.

Frame chairs | **The Faaborg Chair** — Kaare Klint & Carl Petersen

Frame chair for Dansk Kunsthandel

Kaare Klint
1888–1954

year: 1917
materials: Cuban mahogany, wickerwork
prod. by: N.C. Jensen Kjær
inv. no.: A136/1917

After the chair for the Faaborg Museum, Kaare Klint created several variants for oher settings. This chair was used in the art gallery Dansk Kunsthandel, the interior of which Klint designed for Johannes Rump. However, Klint had already designed the chair back in 1916 for Aage Lund's house. The chair appears (and is) heavier than the Faaborg Chair on account of the panel in the back and the extra rail above the seat to hold the seat cushion in place.

Kaare Klint, furniture for Dansk
Kunsthandel (Danish Art Gallery), 1917
(see page 144).

Kaare Klint, furniture for
Thorvaldsens Museum, 1922
(see page 149).

Frame chair for Thorvaldsens Museum

Kaare Klint
1888–1954

year: 1922
materials: Oak burl, wickerwork, leather
prod. by: N.C. Jensen Kjær
inv. no.: 90c/1982

When designing the interior of Thorvaldsen's Museum, Klint revisited the frame chair. This version is even stricter in shape than the Faaborg Chair, which makes it less comfortable. The soft curves of the Faaborg Chair's back rail have now been replaced by circle sections and straight lines. Everything on the chair is linear. It is only the bevelling that prevents the chair from coming across as a purely geometrical exercise.

Klismos chair

Kaj Gottlob
1887–1976

year: 1921
materials: Ash, wickerwork, leather
prod. by: Fritz Hansen
inv. no.: 125/1987

Kaj Gottlob was an architect, but also created many furniture designs. Originally a neoclassicist, he moved towards a modernist expression during the 1930s. Both his architecture and his furniture always featured geometry, frequently circle sections, and personal details. This is also evident in the early, neoclassical furniture for the Frederiksberg Court Building. This *klismos*-type chair stood by a round table in the Court Building's library.

Frame chair

Edvard Thomsen
1884–1980

year: 1930
materials: Ash, beech, textile
inv. no.: 131/1998

Edvard Thomsen, a professor at the Royal Academy of Fine Arts, was mainly an architect, but he also designed furniture. During the 1920s, he created many neoclassical furniture designs, but in this chair we see neoclassicism evolving into functionalism. To make the chair more comfortable, the backrest is high and the armrests have been given horizontal surfaces. The recognition that armrests should consist of horizontal surfaces, while backrests should be vertical, anticipates Hans J. Wegner's Round Chair (see page 160), in which the vertical backrest makes a fluid transition into horizontal, organically shaped armrests.

School chair

Frits Schlegel
1896–1965

year: 1931
materials: Mahogany, beech
prod. by: Fritz Hansen
inv. no.: A36/1931

In this chair, the functionalist architect Fritz Schlegel combined three types: the solid seat is saddle-shaped as on many Windsor chairs; the backrest is large and curved as on the ancient *klismos* chair; while the black-painted undercarriage is made of bentwood beech, as in the Vienna chairs. Schlegel had thus created a more comfortable and exclusive bentwood chair that was also more appropriate as a classroom chair.

The Metropolitan Chair

Aksel Bender Madsen
1916–2000
—
Ejner Larsen
1917–1987

year: 1949
materials: Oak, teak
prod. by: Fritz Hansen
inv. no.: 153/2001

Bender Madsen and Ejner Larsen's frame chair dates from 1949: the year Danish Design made its breakthrough in the United States. It tackles the same theme as Wegner's Round Chair of the same year (see page 160). An almost vertical backrest slides out along the sides, turning into an almost horizontal armrest. The designers applied what was then a brand-new technology: moulded plywood. The legs are conical, thickest where they join the frame that supports the seat. The chair is one of the finest examples of the organic modernism, which emerged internationally in the late 1940s. With its moulded backrest it anticipates later icons such as Arne Jacobsen's Ant Chair (1952) (see page 258).

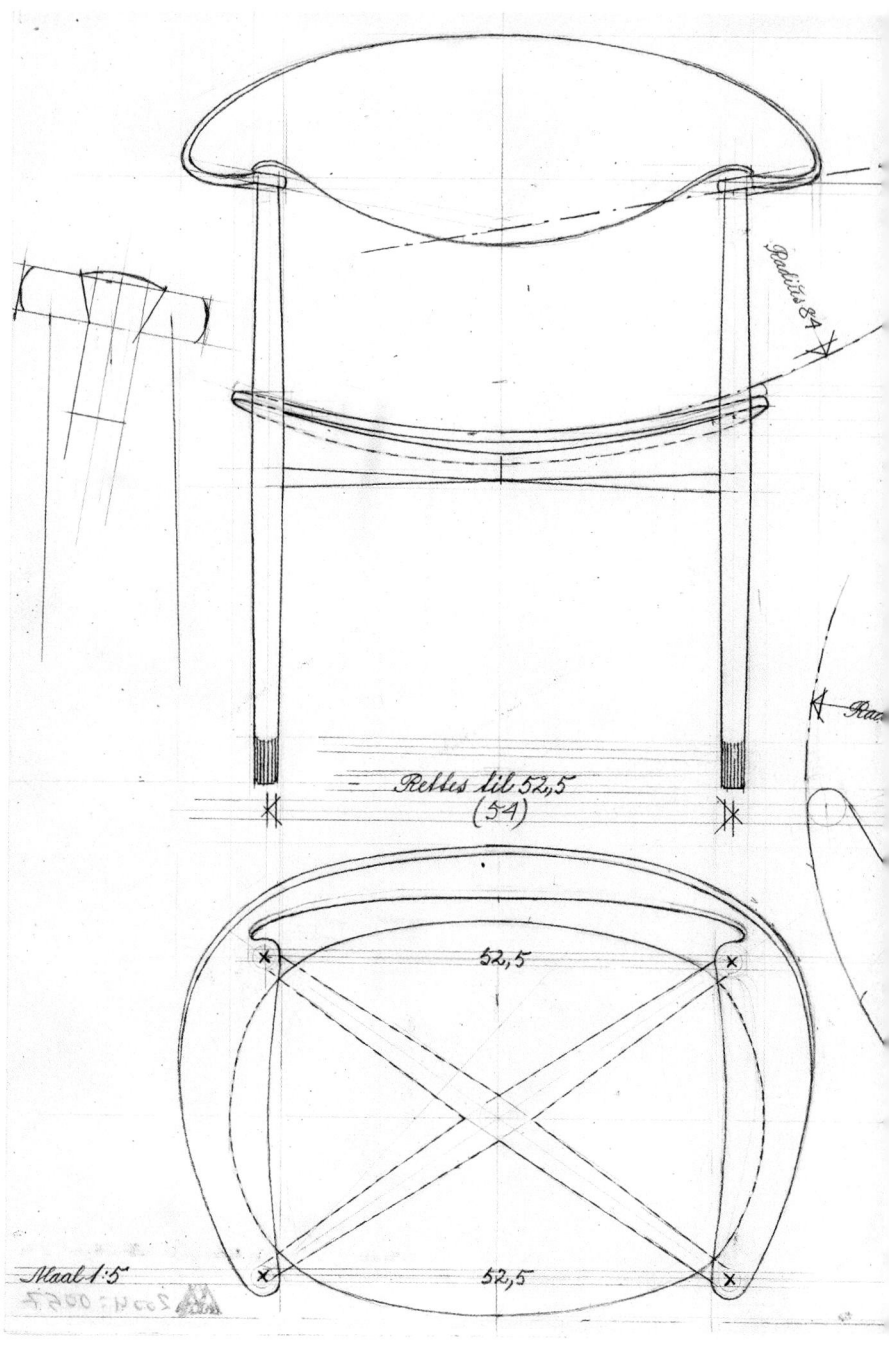

Aksel Bender Madsen and Ejner Larsen,
drawing for the Metropolitan Chair, 1949
(see page 156).

Frame chairs | **The Metropolitan Chair** — Aksel Bender Madsen & Ejner Larsen

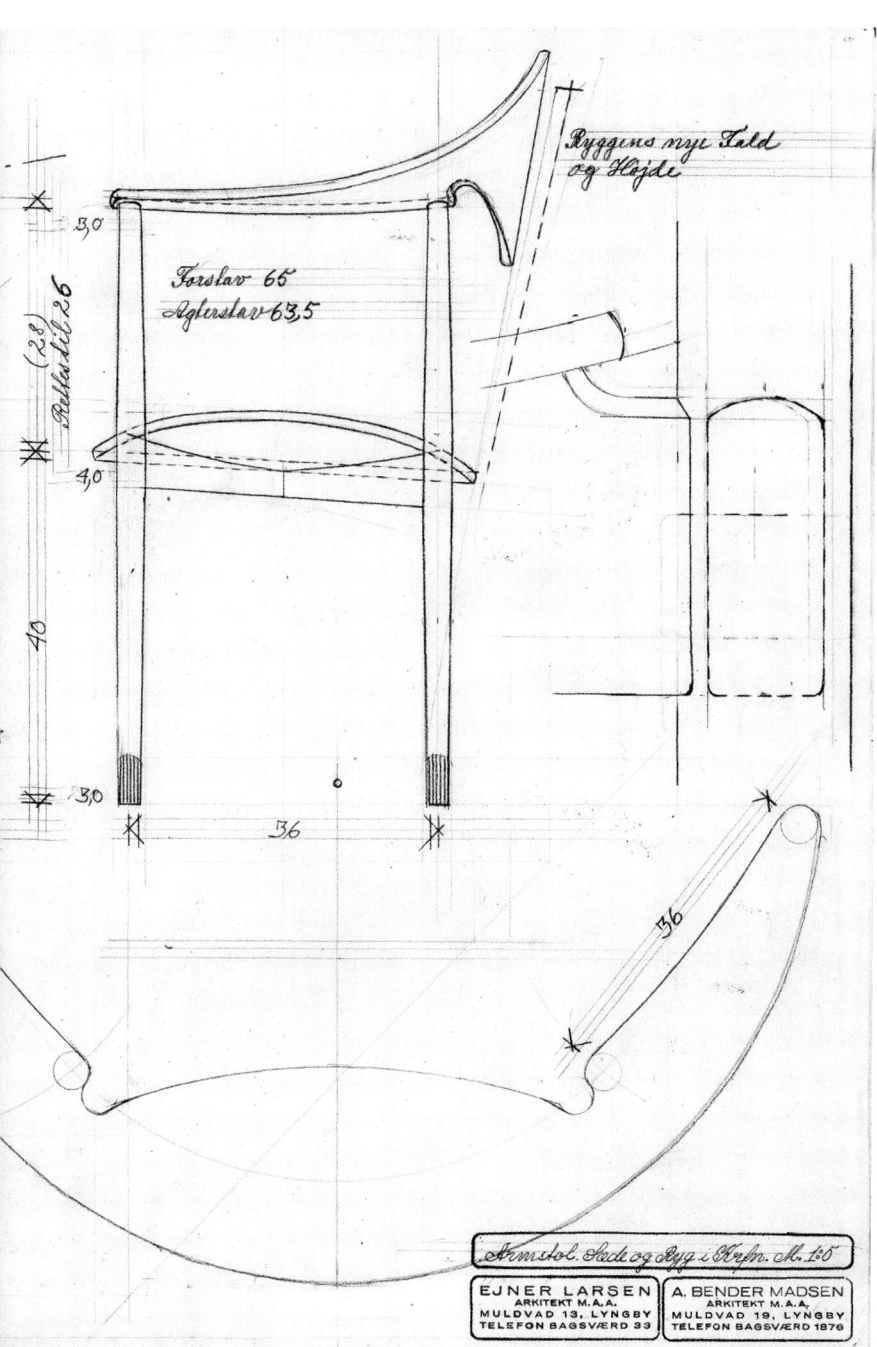

The Chair

Hans J. Wegner
1914–2007

year: 1949
materials: Oak, cane
prod. by: Johannes Hansen Møbelsnedkeri
inv. no.: 84/1952

1949 was the year when American journalists came to Copenhagen and began to write about Danish Design. Wegner's Round Chair was one of their favourites. They referred to it as 'The Chair': the ultimate chair. As far as Wegner was concerned, it was just an ordinary cabinetmaker's chair, which could have been designed long ago. However, it was a reinterpretation of the frame chair and the *klismos* chair (see page 135) as well as a logical extension of Wegner's work on Chinese chairs (see pages 114, 116, 124 and 128). Every element of the chair was organically shaped. The vertical backrest makes a smooth transition into the horizontal armrest, and every detail has its logical justification. The legs are thickest where they are joined to the seat frame. The chair became a symbol of Western democracy when it was used in the first televised presidential debate in the United States, the debate between John F. Kennedy and Richard M. Nixon in 1960.

Cabinetmaker Johannes Hansen's stand at the Copenhagen Cabinetmakers' Guild's furniture exhibition, 1952. Dining room set designed by Hans J. Wegner.

The Cow Horn Chair

Hans J. Wegner
1914–2007

year:	1952
materials:	Hickory, rosewood
prod. by:	Johannes Hansen Møbelsnedkeri
inv. no.:	65/1953

Personally, Wegner did not consider The Chair (see page 160) the ultimate chair, and throughout his career he continued his attempts to design a better chair. His effort resulted in about 500 chairs. In 1952, he presented the Cow Horn Chair, which stands out by being open and by the fact that, unlike The Chair, it can be pushed in under a table. The 'horns' provide comfortable support for the elbows. Wegner also discovered that a chair's expressive potential lay in its top rail. The inlays in the back rail serve to join the two pieces of wood together. They provide a large surface for gluing, thus making the chair strong.

Swivel chair

Hans J. Wegner
1914–2007

year: 1955
materials: Oak, steel, leather
prod. by: Johannes Hansen Møbelsnedkeri
inv. no.: 195/2005

The consultant doctor Eigil Snorrason, who conducted research into sitting positions, criticised Danish-designed chairs for providing poor lumbar support. However, he praised Wegner's Cow Horn Chair (see page 163) as offering better lumbar support than most. Snorrason and Wegner began collaborating and developed an office chair with lower lumbar support. This solution also looked better when the chair was standing next to a desk. The office chair turned into an organic sculpture, in which a top rail, consisting of five pieces of wood glued together, is suspended in a light steel frame. The hard, cold, anonymous steel encounters the soft, warm, tactile wood. Craftsmanship and industry fused into one.

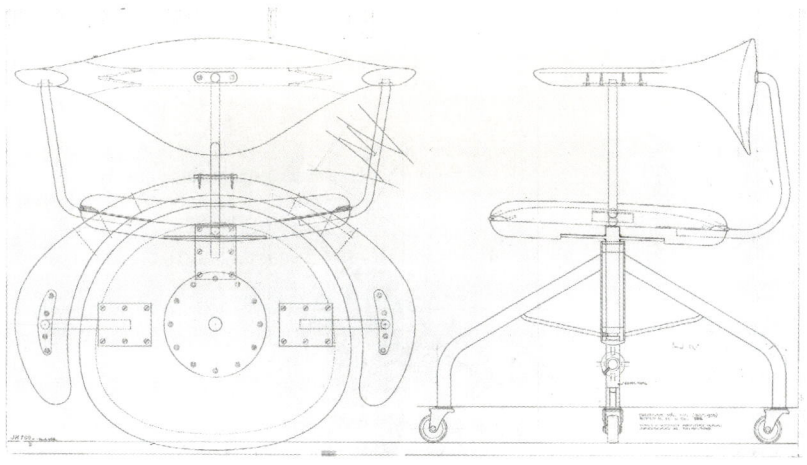

Hans J. Wegner, drawing of JH502, 1955.

JH701

Hans J. Wegner
1914–2007

year:	1965
materials:	Maple, rosewood, steel tubes
prod. by:	Johannes Hansen Møbelsnedkeri
inv. no.:	140/1990

This frame chair was Wegner's favourite, designed for his own dining table at home. The chair is light and simple, yet complex. The simple steel frame supports the thin top rail, which provides exactly the right support for the back to accommodate the right lumbar curvature. The four parts of the top rail are joined together with inlaid wood, providing a larger surface for the glue and consequently greater strength. In contrast to the back, the chair's armrests are horizontally aligned with the table, which the chair is easily pulled up to. The use of a steel frame highlights the sculptural quality of the top rail.

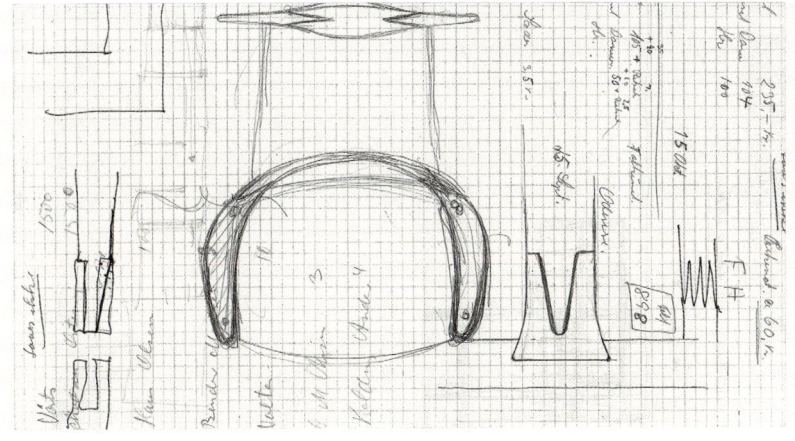

Hans J. Wegner's sketch
of the top rail of JH701.

PP63

Hans J. Wegner
1914–2007

year:	1975
materials:	Ash, wengé, paper yarn
prod. by:	PP Møbler
inv. no.:	198/1987

In Wegner's late chairs he departed from the organic shapes that had earned him world fame. He focused on simplifying the manufacturing process without, however, compromising on the expressiveness of the top rail. PP63 is a broad, majestic version of Wegner's PP62, which was made of vertical poles that were flattened where they were joined together. The chair has a more geometric and static expression. The inlaid wood in the top rail is not only for decoration but provides a larger surface for glueing. It also makes slight variations in grain less noticeable.

Frame chair

Ole Wanscher
1903–1985

year:	1960
materials:	Cherry, textile
prod. by:	P. Jeppesens Møbelfabrik A/S
inv. no.:	50/1981

Kaare Klint's successor as Professor of Furniture, Ole Wanscher, designed several frame chairs. This the lightest, and with its round, outward-sweeping armrests, it probably relates more to Chinese chairs than to the new neoclassical tradition, of which Kaare Klint's frame chairs are such excellent examples.

8002, Chair for Café Victor

The chair was created at a time when café life was taking off in Denmark. It was used at Café Victor in Copenhagen. The chair was a result of the designers' in-depth study of laminated wood and intended as a new take on the most successful café chair in the world: Thonet's bentwood chair, No. 14 (see page 84). The fact that it can be stacked is not the only improvement. It also solves the bentwood chair's greatest weakness: the joining of the seat and the legs, which usually requires a bolt. Here, the laminated legs are pressed into the seat frame with a wedge-shaped pin, which, after the application of aqueous glue, expands inside a conical hole. The resulting structure is extremely strong.

Rud Thygesen
1932-2019
—
Johnny Sørensen
1944-

year:	1980
materials:	Beech, laminated linoleum, leather
prod. by:	Magnus Olesen A/S
inv. no.:	90/1986

Café Victor in Copenhagen with Rud Thygesen's chair, early 1980s.

Frame chairs | **8002, Chair for Café Victor** — Rud Thygesen & Johnny Sørensen

Chair no. 10, Skagen

Jørgen Gammelgaard
1938–1991

year: 1985
materials: Steel tube, wood
prod. by: Schiang Collection
inv. no.: 113/1986

Jørgen Gammelgaard succeeded Poul Kjærholm as Professor of Furniture Design at the Royal Danish Academy of Fine Arts. Like Kjærholm, he was an advocate of reduction and, as here, of traditional furniture types but he was also intrigued by new methods of production. This modern, industrial frame chair combines a 1980s take on the classic frame chair with a cool, minimalist structure. The light seat and top rail of the chair have a floating expression. The supporting and supported elements are separated, despite the slender character of the construction.

English chairs

English 18th-century furniture design represents a golden age in international design history and has served as inspiration in many other countries. The chairs of the English upper middle class were taken up in Denmark as early as ca. 1800, and during the first half of the 20th century, many Danish cabinetmakers created English-style furniture for Danish dining rooms.

The main source of influence, however, was Professor Kaare Klint's studies of English furniture design. In his opinion, the specific details of the old Chippendale chairs could be ignored, but 'all the utilitarian aspects are resolved in exemplary fashion. Seat height, width, depth; everything is as it should be. The back offers support where it is needed, and so forth.' In his assessment, the chairs in many regards lived up to what was required of satisfactory furniture in Klint's time. Klint's chair for Designmuseum Danmark (see p. 182) became a model for many of his students, who continued to develop the type. Klint regarded the chair as contemporary and considered the undercarriage a cost-efficient solution. Obviously, given the insistence on top craftsmanship and the finest materials, such as Cuban mahogany, the chairs hardly lived up to the intended social ambitions. Hence, the English-inspired furniture was reserved for the upper middle class, also in Denmark.

178	Chair, Jens Brøtterup
180	Chippendale chair
182	The Red Chair, Kaare Klint
184	Chair for Prime Minister Stauning, Kaare Klint
188	Chair for Kvinderegensen, Rigmor Andersen
192	Chair, Børge Mogensen & Lis Ahlmann
194	Dining room chair, Ole Wanscher
196	Ladder-back chair
200	Ladder-back chair, Ole Wanscher

Chair

Jens Brøtterup
ca. 1752–1832

year: 1794–1803
materials: Mahogany, horsehair
inv. no.: A29/1926

The fondness of Danish cabinetmakers and furniture designers for English furniture design dates back a long way. Jens Brøtterup had worked in England for six years as a cabinetmaker. This spindle-back chair is so simple that it could be serially manufactured. Consequently, its expression anticipates the ideals of Danish furniture design of the early 20th century.

Chippendale chair

England

year: ca. 1750
materials: Mahogany
inv. no.: B135a-b/1930

On account of its excellent craftsmanship and simple, expedient shapes, English furniture design was a model for many Danish furniture designers, particularly the students of Kaare Klint. Designmuseum Danmark owns a series of pattern books by the famous English cabinetmakers Chippendale, Hepplewhite and Sheraton, which the Danish designers studied. Like the Chinese, the English regarded the back of the chair as the domain of artistic expression, a view that many Danish furniture designers were also aware of. The ornamental openwork backs of the 18th century were intended to lend the dining chair a vibrant expression when the room was empty, while the undercarriage was always more plain.

The Red Chair

Kaare Klint
1888–1954

year: 1927
materials: Cuban mahogany, Morocco leather
prod. by: Rud. Rasmussens Snedkerier
inv. no.: 328/1989

Professor Kaare Klint's chair for Designmuseum Danmark's lecture theatre is the best-known example of his working method. He believed that historic furniture could be reused, in part or in whole, if its construction lived up to the constructional demands of the modern age. He asked his student Ole Wanscher to measure a Chippendale chair at the National Gallery of Denmark and used its undercarriage, adding a more comfortable backrest from another chair. The chair was presented at the 1929 Barcelona International Exposition; the same year that German designer Mies van der Rohe presented his Barcelona Chair (see page 39).

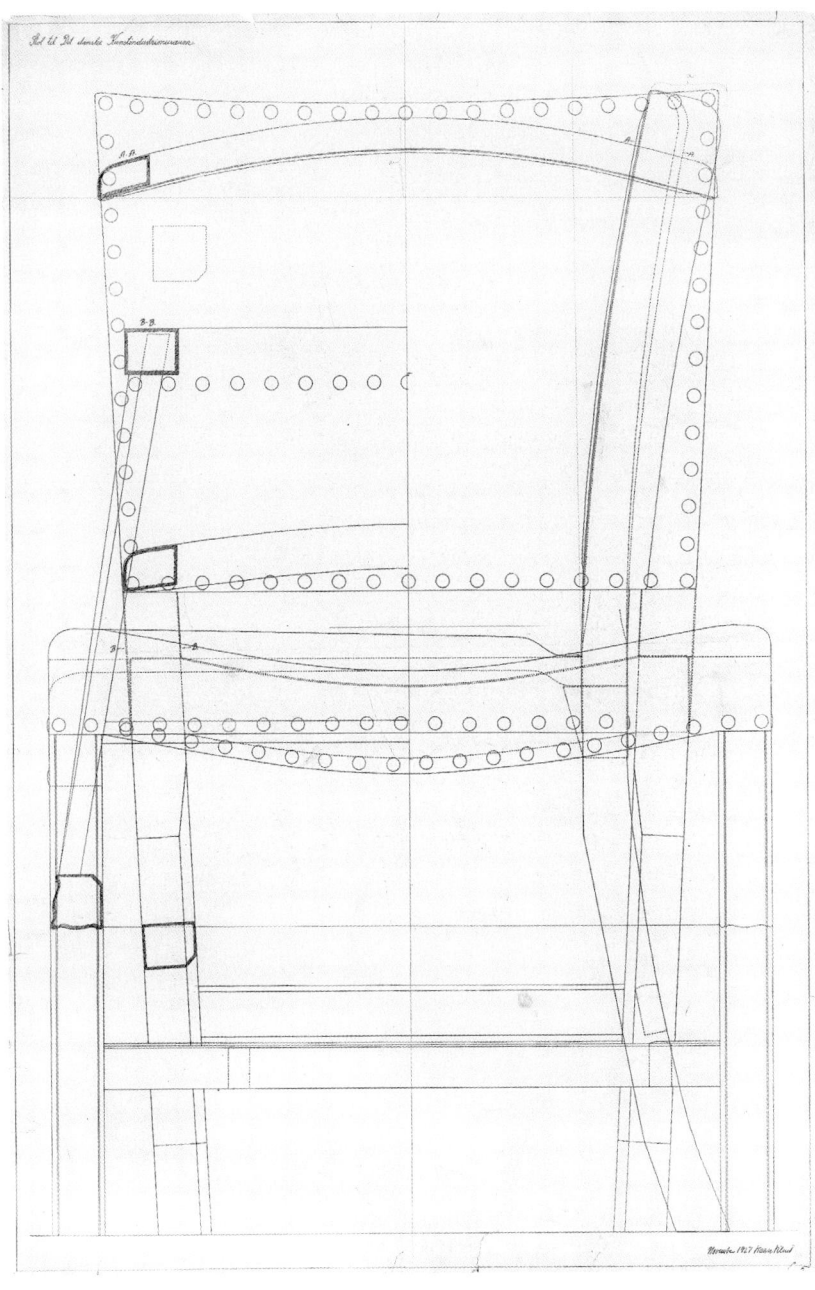

Kaare Klint's drawing of
the Red Chair, 1927.

Chair for Prime Minister Stauning

Kaare Klint
1888–1954

year: 1930
materials: Mahogany, horsehair
prod. by: Rud. Rasmussens Snedkerier
inv. no.: D1512c

The social democrat Thorvald Stauning is regarded as the founder of the Danish welfare state. He had been a cigar sorter before he became a politician and had furnished his home with charming, historicist furniture. However, when it came to designing his office in the Prime Minister's Department, he contacted Kaare Klint, who had recently designed Designmuseum Danmark (see page 182). Klint designed all the furniture for the office. Ministers were given the same chairs as the ones Klint had designed for Designmuseum Danmark, albeit with armrests, just as Stauning's own chair was also larger.

English chairs | **Chair for Prime Minister Stauning** – Kaare Klint

Prime Minister Thorvald Stauning in his office at the Prime Minister's Department with Kaare Klint's chairs (see page 185).

English chairs | **Chair for Prime Minister Stauning** – Kaare Klint

Chair for Kvinderegensen

Rigmor Andersen
1903–1995

year: 1931
materials: Mahogany, leather
prod. by: Rud. Rasmussens Snedkerier
inv. no.: 45/1999

The first university hall of residence for women, Kvinderegensen, was built on Amager Boulevard in Copenhagen in 1932. Professor Kaare Klint was asked to recommend a talented female furniture designer to be responsible for furnishing the hall. The task fell to Rigmor Andersen, one of Klint's first students and his close collaborator, who designed all the furniture for Kvinderegensen. The chair for the ceremonial hall is a reinterpretation of Kaare Klint's chair for Designmuseum Danmark (see page 182). It is slightly simplified and reduced in size and also has a lighter look. The chair is still used for celebrations in the hall of residence, which is now also open to male students.

The assembly hall at Kvinderegensen (university hall of residence for women), in the 1930s with furniture designed by Rigmor Andersen (see page 188).

English chairs | **Chair for Kvinderegensen** – Rigmor Andersen

Chair

Børge Mogensen
1914–1972
—
Lis Ahlmann
1894–1979

year:	1941
materials:	Oak, textile
prod. by:	Ove Lander
inv. no.:	77/1947

Børge Mogensen made this early chair with armrests while he was still working for his teacher, Kaare Klint. The inspiration from the master's Red Chair (see page 182) is evident, but Mogensen's chair is simpler and hence cheaper. The upholstery was made by the leading fabric designer of the day, Lis Ahlmann, who had collaborated with Kaare Klint and Mogens Koch. However, it was her collaboration with Børge Mogensen in the mid 20th century that made her Denmark's leading furniture fabric designer. As in this chair, she was often inspired by simple patterns of traditional weaving.

Dining room chair

Ole Wanscher
1903–1985

year: 1943
materials: Rosewood, beech, leather
prod. by: A.J. Iversen
inv. no.: B56/1943

Ole Wanscher was a student of Kaare Klint and succeeded him as Professor of Furniture Design at the Royal Danish Academy of Fine Arts. He was also a leading furniture historian. His interest in the history of furniture extended well beyond what he could incorporate structurally and functionally in his design of new furniture. He sought to understand the shapes of historic furniture. This is evident in his own designs, in which he refines lines and details, achieving great elegance and expression. This interpretation of an English dining chair is an excellent example of Wanscher's talent as a designer to invest well-known types with an innovative lightness.

Ladder-back chair

England

year: ca. 1770
materials: Mahogany
inv. no.: B11/1934

English furniture from the 18th century provided a rich source of inspiration for Danish furniture designers during the 20th century, in part because of the excellent craftsmanship and rational design. The ladder-back chair is actually a primitive traditional type that extends far back in history, but the English had refined the horizontal slats between the straight back posts to create an extremely elegant, intricate flow of lines.

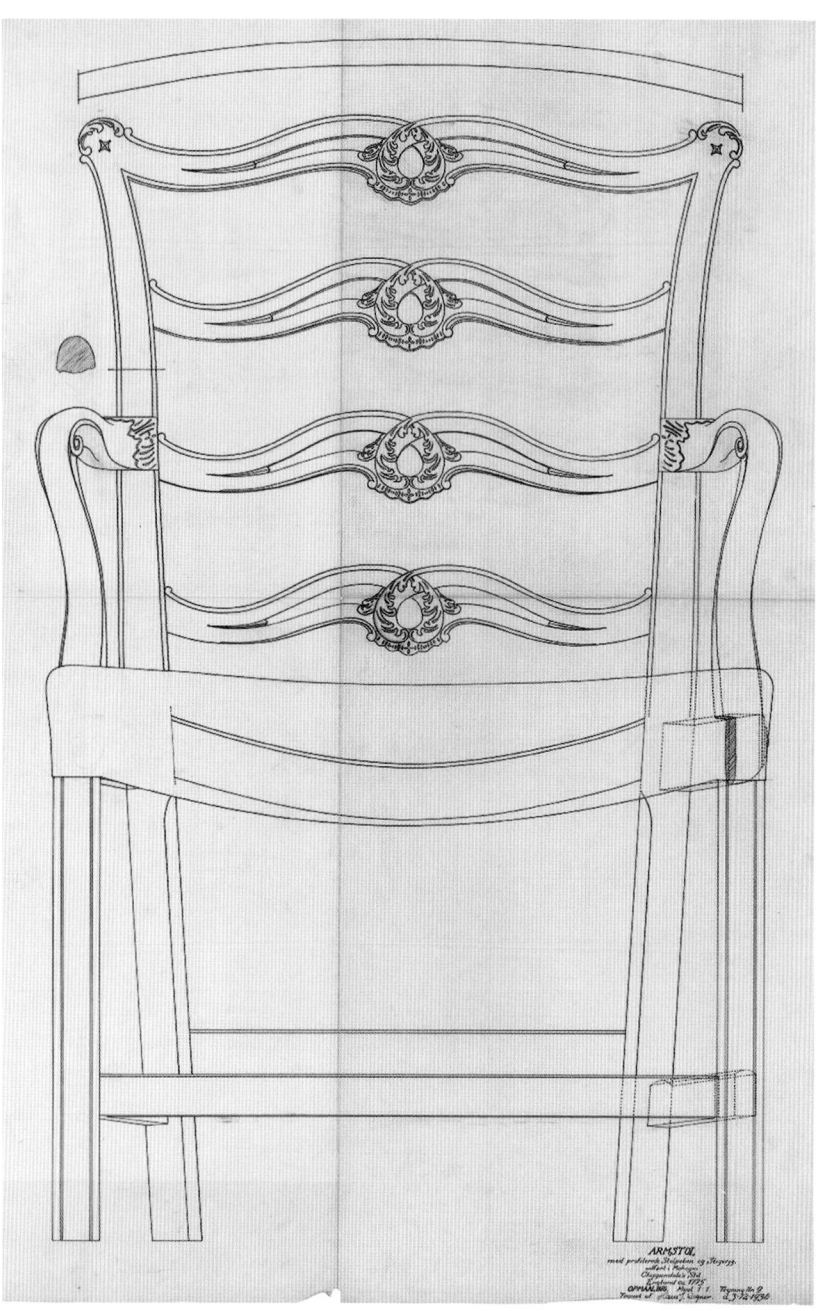

Designmuseum Danmark's English ladder-back chair (see page 196), measured by furniture design student Hans J. Wegner, 1937–1938.

Ole Wanscher's ladder-back chair,
1940s, (see page 201).

English chairs | **Ladder-back chair** – Ole Wanscher

Ladder-back chair

Ole Wanscher
1903–1985

year: ca. 1946
materials: Beech
prod. by: Fritz Hansen
inv. no.: 81/2010

The furniture historian and Professor of Furniture Ole Wanscher attempted to reinterpret the English ladder-back chair (see page 196) for Fritz Hansen. He was fascinated by elegant lines and succeeded in transferring something of the refinement of the English chair to the simple, affordable everyday chair. It is a typical example of the Danish furniture school's ambition of adapting excellent historical designs to the current time.

Windsor chairs

When designers set out to make affordable furniture for the new Danish welfare state in the 20th century, they regarded the Windsor chair type as an exemplary mass-produced chair that did not require advanced industrial manufacturing equipment. The chair had been common in Scandinavia since the 19th century.

When the Windsor chair was originally introduced in the 18th century, it was the first example of a distributed labour process, where the different components of the chair were made by different cabinetmakers and subsequently assembled by others in an approach anticipating rational, industrial production based on standard components. The delicate spindles that make up the back and the legs are attached to a solid saddle seat. The different parts are often made of different types of wood, depending on their form and function. Two types in particular are common in Danish furniture design: the comb-back and the bow-back. The comb-back type has a top rail where the spindles form a frame, while the bow-back type has a bentwood back brace. The chairs' light, transparent look was a good match for the modernist visions of bright, hygienic homes.

204	——	Windsor chair
206	——	Chair for Nyborg Library, Hans J. Wegner
208	——	J52, Børge Mogensen
212	——	Windsor chair, Børge Mogensen
214	——	Windsor chair, Ole Wanscher
216	——	Windsor chair, Hans J. Wegner
218	——	PP112, Hans J. Wegner
220	——	Mikado III, Johannes Foersom & Peter Hiort-Lorenzen
222	——	PP550, the Peacock Chair, Hans J. Wegner

Windsor chair

England

year: 1850–1860
materials: Beech, ash, maple
inv. no.: B9/1934

Simple spindle-back and slatted furniture plays an important role in Danish functionalism. Since there was no industrial manufacturing until after the Second World War, the English Windsor chair was a key model. It emerged in England during the 18th century and was the first chair to be produced in a rational process, where the manufacture of the individual elements was carried out by various specialists. This was a precursor of industrial mass production. In Denmark, this spartan, anonymous type was regarded as an affordable, practical, timeless chair. Designmuseum Danmark's Windsor type was a standard item on the furniture design curriculum.

Chair for Nyborg Library

Hans J. Wegner
1914–2007

year: 1938–1940
materials: Maple, leather
inv. no.: 140a-b/1993

While Wegner attended the School of Arts and Crafts, which shared premises with Designmuseum Danmark, one of the assignments was to analyse the museum's Windsor chair (see page 204). Wegner did so well that, even before completing his studies, he was employed by Flemming Lassen and Erik Møller. Here, he designed furniture for Nyborg Library, which was one of the firm's architectural projects. As a result of Wegner's study of Windsor chairs in the Museum, the library in Nyborg was furnished with spindle-back chairs. Wegner simplified the chair and left out the decorative details, thus giving the chair a more contemporary expression.

J52

Børge Mogensen
1914–1972

year: 1944
materials: Beech
prod. by: FDB
inv. no.: 243/1990

In 1942, Børge Mogensen was appointed head of the furniture design studio of the Confederation of Danish Manufacturing and Retail Cooperatives (FDB), the purpose of which was to design affordable, high-quality furniture for a broad Danish audience. As a student, Børge Mogensen had analysed the Design Museum's 18th-century Windsor chair (see page 204) and had even made an exact replica of it. For FDB, he simplified the type and, in contrast to the English chairs, made it in a single type of wood: Danish beech, which was cheap and could be steam-bent. The type is known as a comb-back, as the spindles in the back form a comb shape.

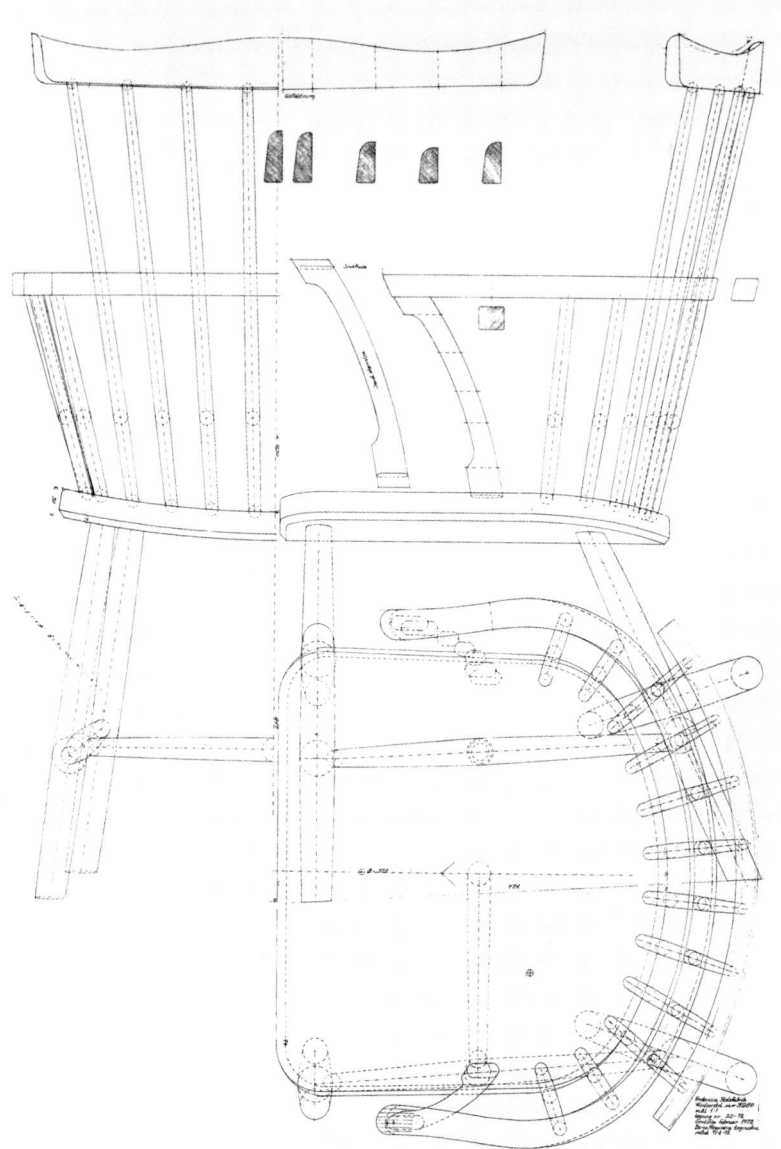

Børge Mogensen, drawing of the popular J52 from FDB, 1944 (see page 208).

FDB exhibition photo with furniture by Børge Mogensen, including the Spindle-Back Chair (see page 212).

Windsor chair

Børge Mogensen
1914–1972

year: 1942–1950
materials: Beech
prod. by: FDB
inv. no.: 246/1997

Børge Mogensen and several of the later heads of the furniture studio of tthe Confederation of Danish Manufacturing and Retail Cooperatives (FDB) designed variations on the Windsor chair theme. The chairs were extremely common in Danish homes during the post-war years. After 2000, FDB (now COOP) revived the chair, which enjoys renewed popularity.

Windsor chair

Ole Wanscher
1903–1985

year: 1942
materials: Beech, elm
prod. by: Fritz Hansen
inv. no.: 66/1994

During the mid 20th century, most Danish furniture designers designed at least one version of the Windsor chair. The furniture historian, Professor of Furniture Ole Wanscher chose one of the more complex types with the characteristic, structural V-shape in the back. His furniture is always characterised by a particular elegance in its lines and detailing. Wegner was also fascinated by this V-type chair and designed a V-type Windsor chair at the same time as designing his Wishbone Chair (see page 117).

Windsor chair

Hans J. Wegner
1914–2007

year: 1949
materials: Teak, oak
prod. by: Fritz Hansen
inv. no.: 242/1989

In this small, refined, minimalist spindle-back chair, Wegner reduced the number of spindles in comparison to traditional spindle-back chairs. The thickness of the poles in the back has been increased at the structure's joints, as in his Peacock Chair (see page 222). 'The wood should be present where it's needed, and only there.'

PP112

Hans J. Wegner
1914–2007

year: 1978
materials: Ash
prod. by: PP Møbler
inv. no.: 267/1989

Wegner continued to design Windsor chairs throughout his career. In this late chair, the spindle-back theme encounters two of Wegner's other favourite types, as the PP112 also has a backrest that embraces the seated person, like a comb-back chair, and a sloping back brace reminiscent of the Chinese chairs.

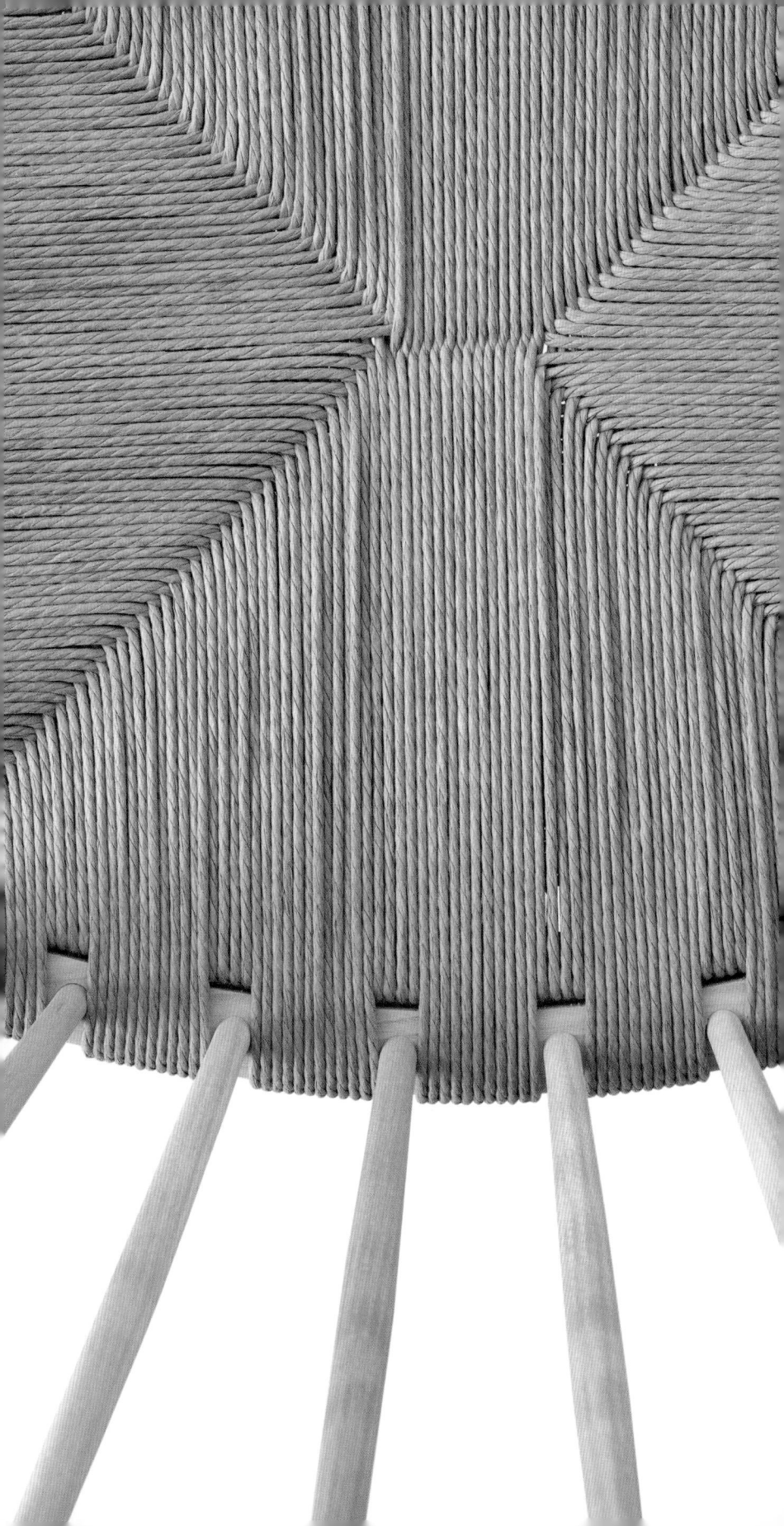

Mikado III

Johannes Foersom
1947-
—
Peter Hiort-Lorenzen
1943-

year:	1996
materials:	Beech, hickory
prod. by:	Kvist Møbler
inv. no.:	100/2002

Although Mikado refers to the game of pick-up-sticks, the chair really represents a continuation of the long tradition for Windsor chairs. As in Windsor chairs, the seat is solid, and the legs are anchored in a hole in the seat with a wedge that is knocked down into the leg. As in Wegner's Peacock Chair (see page 222), Foersom and Hiort-Lorenzen chose to let the wedge remain visible by using a dark wood. The visually innovative elements is the fact that the chair has no top rail; nothing holds the spindles together in the back, and they are simply allowed to 'bristle'. This gives the chair a simpler and more expressive appearance.

PP550, The Peacock Chair

Hans J. Wegner
1914–2007

year: 1947
materials: Ash, teak, paper yarn
prod. by: PP Møbler
inv. no.: 197/1987

The Peacock Chair marks a turning point in Wegner's work and in the development of Danish furniture design. The theme of the Windsor chair was so popular because the chair was rational in terms of use and production. With the Peacock Chair, however, Wegner demonstrated that it could also be a poetic and highly expressive item of furniture. Even though the chair is decorative, every part of its structure has a rational explanation. The flattened sections of the vertical spindles that form the backrest make the chair comfortable. The teak armrests do not show any discoloration from daily use and age. It was Wegner's colleague Finn Juhl who dubbed it the Peacock Chair, and because of its powerful graphic expression, it was used as a logo for Danish Modern.

Shell chairs

The shell type originated outside Denmark during the 20th century, driven by new technologies for working with metal, wood and plastic. It is characterised by single- or double-curvature elements used to form the back and seat. Most seat and support shells rest on light, delicate constructions. The shell dominates the chair's expression – it aims for a weightless look and often has a sculptural expression. Shell chairs have their real breakthrough with organic post-war modernism and take the modernist ideal of reductionism one step further, as the shells make it possible to minimise the number of components.

In Denmark, the capacity for moulding double-curvature shells in laminated wood is introduced during the 1940s, and Denmark stands out especially within the simplification and sophistication of this shell type. Initially, with traditional cabinetmaker's techniques, new steam-bending technology and new plywood technology, but as early as in 1952, Arne Jacobsen's Ant Chair, the first Danish industrial chair, sets a new standard for simplicity and reduction in the number of components for this furniture type.

226	——	Chair
228	——	The Landi Chair, Hans Coray
230	——	DSR, Charles Eames & Ray Eames
232	——	The Tulip Chair, Eero Saarinen
234	——	EKC9, Poul Kjærholm
236	——	The Portex Chair, Peter Hvidt & Orla Mølgaard-Nielsen
238	——	LCW, Charles Eames & Ray Eames
240	——	FH1936, Hans J. Wegner
244	——	Shell Chair, Børge Mogensen
246	——	The AX Chair, Peter Hvidt & Orla Mølgaard-Nielsen
250	——	Prototype, Poul Kjærholm
252	——	Shell chair, Søren Hansen
254	——	3107, the Series 7 Chair, Arne Jacobsen
258	——	3100, the Ant, Arne Jacobsen
260	——	3105, the Mosquito, Arne Jacobsen
264	——	3102, the Tongue, Arne Jacobsen
266	——	4130, Grand Prix, Arne Jacobsen
270	——	3103, Arne Jacobsen
272	——	3208, the Seagull, Arne Jacobsen
276	——	The Bow Chair, Grete Jalk
278	——	The two-part shell chair, prototype, Hans J. Wegner
282	——	NXT, Peter Karpf
284	——	Trinidad, Nanna Ditzel
286	——	Rex, Christina Strand
290	——	Gubi, Komplot Design

Chair

year:	ca. 1860–1870
materials:	Papier mâché, lacquer, gilding
prod. by:	Emil Meyers Fabrik
inv. no.:	B166a-b/1930

J. Emil Meyer used papier mâché for this shell chair. The chair was fashioned in one piece, with no visible joints; something that later designers spent many years trying to replicate. Thus, the chair anticipates the shell chairs of the 20th century. In the 1860s, papier mâché was popular as a cheap substitute material in the production of furniture and decorative objects, although its malleability was not used to create new designs. Designers tended to copy existing, neo-rococo shapes, and this chair borrowed shapes from Gebrüder Thonet's bentwood chairs (see page 84).

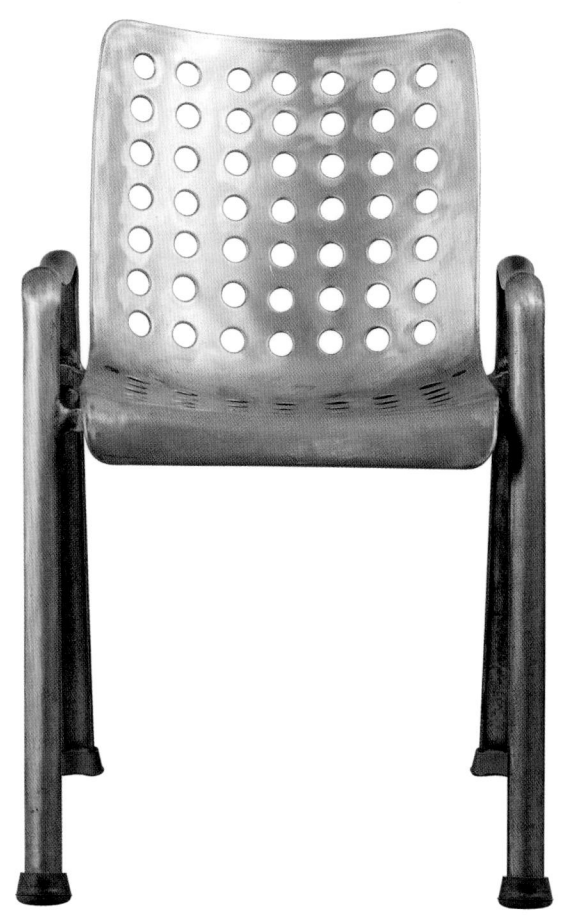

The Landi Chair

Hans Coray (CH)
1906–1991

year: 1938
materials: Aluminium, rubber
producent: P. & W. Blattmann Metallwaren-Fabrik
inv. no.: 110a/1995

The Swiss artist and furniture designer's best-known design is this minimalist, lightweight aluminium shell chair. The Landi Chair was designed for the national Landesausstellung (National Exhibition) in Zurich, Switzerland (1939). The seat and back of this stacking chair are moulded from a single piece of aluminium, into which large holes have been cut. The chair can be used both indoors and out. The frame is made of bent aluminium tubing, which also forms the legs and armrests. In 1970, production was resumed, and in 2004 the chair's iconic status was celebrated on a Swiss postage stamp. In 2016, Vitra again resumed production of the chair.

DSR

Charles Eames (US)
1907–1978
—
Ray Eames (US)
1912–1988

year:	1950
materials:	Fibreglass, steel
prod. by:	Herman Miller
inv. no.:	82/1957

The couple Charles and Ray Eames conducted early experiments with new techniques and approaches to design. The Plastic Shell Group was an early example of 'customising', where the customer was offered a range of options besides colour. The series consisted of two organically shaped, fibreglass-reinforced plastic shells, which could be fitted with three different metal rod undercarriages. The series, which is still in production, now include this dining chair (Dining Height Side Chair Rod Base), the armchair (LAR) and the rocking chair (RAR).

The Tulip Chair

Eero Saarinen (FI-US)
1910–1961

year:	1955–1956
materials:	Polyester, aluminum, textile
prod. by:	Knoll
inv. no.:	249a/1992

Eero Saarinen and Charles Eames designed several items of shell furniture together, but Saarinen was the first designer to devote himself to creating a chair in one piece. This chair is part of his Pedestal Series, in which the traditional four legs became a single central leg. The Tulip Chair is an organic shape, in which the seat shell is a seamless extension of the leg. The leg is moulded from aluminium, and the fibreglass seat is reinforced with polyester, since it was not technically possible to create an entire chair in a single piece. It was not until much later that Verner Panton succeeded with his Panton Chair (see page 318).

EKC9

Poul Kjærholm
1929–1980

year:	1960
materials:	Steel, fibreglass, leather
prod. by:	E. Kold Christensen
inv. no.:	75/1961

The chair's three legs are curved like the legs on Abildgaard's *klismos* chair (see page 135), but here they have been consolidated into a single leg, resulting in a springy pedestal. The seat is upholstered in whole pieces of leather, shaped by the gentle pressure of sandbags over many weeks. The chair's seat acquired its shape from an impression in sand of Poul Kjærholm's wife, Hanne Kjærholm. Like much of Kjærholm's furniture, the chair was originally produced by E. Kold Christensen. Later, Fritz Hansen took over production and changed the name to PK9.

The Portex Chair

Peter Hvidt
1916–1986

—

Orla Mølgaard-Nielsen
1907–1993

year: 1945
materials: Plywood, beech, teak
prod. by: Fritz Hansen
inv. no.: 83a-b/1994

The name of the series, Portex, is an anagram of the word 'export' and is also the title of an ambitious post-war collaboration between Danish furniture manufacturers. For example, Fritz Hansen Eftf. manufactured the chair, and Carl Hansen & Søn the bookcase. The series also included armchairs, tables, beds and cabinets intended for furnishing the homes of families impacted by the war. The details of the chairs were partly inspired by American Shaker furniture (see page 59) and made use of the latest wood-bending techniques. The chair can be stacked, and the other items are knock-down structures, meaning they can easily be taken apart and flat-packed for transport.

LCW

Charles Eames (US)
1907–1978
—
Ray Eames (US)
1912–1988

year:	1946
materials:	Olive, ash
prod. by:	Herman Miller Furniture Company
inv. no.:	81/1957

In 1946, the Eames couple were the first designers to apply 3D moulding of plywood to furniture production. The technique was developed for the Allies' Mosquito aircraft during the Second World War. In 1942, plywood was used for leg splints for wounded soldiers. After the war, the Eameses refined the technique, producing a series of 3D chair shells, which were so comfortable that padding was unnecessary. This chair is a lounge chair, in which the two wooden shells are attached by rubber buffers to a bent frame. The chair was designed for industrial mass production and quickly acquired iconic status.

FH1936

Hans J. Wegner
1914–2007

year:	1948
materials:	Teak, beech
prod. by:	Fritz Hansen
inv. no.:	82/1989

FH1936 was launched at the 1936 Cabinetmakers' Autumn Exhibition at Designmuseum Danmark. It was one of the earliest Danish moulded plywood chairs. The chair's two oval plywood shells are so thin that they appear to be floating. They had a one-directional curvature and were fitted on to a traditional solid beechwood frame. This shell chair was part of a series including a sofa with double-sized shells and a small coffee table. The chair and the sofa were a huge export success, especially in England. Wegner designed several variations on the shell-chair theme, including CH07, CH22, CH23 and CH33. The climax was probably the three-part shell chair, which was never put into production.

Hans J. Wegner, FH1936 (see page 240)
with matching table and sofa,
designed for Fritz Hansen, 1948.

Cabinetmaker Erhard Rasmussen's stand at the Copenhagen Cabinetmakers' Guild's furniture exhibition, 1949. Furniture designed by Børge Mogensen, including his Shell Chair (see page 244).

Shell chairs | **Shell Chair** – Børge Mogensen

Shell Chair

Børge Mogensen
1914–1972

year: 1949
materials: Maple
prod. by: Erhard Rasmussen
inv. no.: 74a-b/2013

Børge Mogensen designed this chair for the 1949 Copenhagen Cabinetmakers' Guild's furniture exhibition. The exhibition became the international breakthrough of Danish furniture design, and Mogensen also made a name for himself. The chair's playful, sculptural design differs from Mogensen's other work, in which inspiration from the rational, matter-of-fact Klint school is much more evident. In this chair he applies the latest technology of the time – moulded plywood – for which Arne Jacobsen, among others, became famous some years later.

The AX Chair

Peter Hvidt
1916–1986
—
Orla Mølgaard-Nielsen
1907–1993

year:	1950
materials:	Plywood, beech, mahogany
prod. by:	Fritz Hansen
inv. no.:	159/1950

The architect duo Hvidt & Mølgaard's Portex series was an impressive concept (see page 236). Five years later they designed AX, a less ambitious range of tables and chairs. AX was a combination of laminated rails for the arms and legs and 3D-moulded seat shells. As in a tennis reacket, the core of the legs was solid mahogany. The furniture could be flat-packed for transport (long before IKEA) and became a resounding success in England and the United States. For the launch at Designmuseum Danmark, the chair was upholstered in leather and wool, reversible to suit the season.

Peter Hvidt and Orla Mølgaard-Nielsen, AX Chair (see page 247), designed for Fritz Hansen, flat-packed for transport.

Poul Kjærholm, drawing of prototype
for Fritz Hansen, 1952 (see page 250).

Prototype

Poul Kjærholm
1929–1980

year: 1952
materials: Plywood
prod. by: Fritz Hansen
inv. no.: 34/2011

PK0 was one of the first chairs that Poul Kjærholm designed after completing his training as a furniture architect. In the design he pushed the moulding technique to its absolute limits, thus also challenging the conventional notion of chair design. The two 3D-curvature shells were fixed to a curved frame with just three legs, which made the chair light and organic. Due to the extreme curvature of the plywood, the chair was never put into mass production, unlike Arne Jacobsen's Ant Chair (see page 258), which was designed at the same time as PK0.
A limited edition of PK0s was produced in 1997 to celebrate the 125th anniversary of the Fritz Hansen company.

Shell chair

Søren Hansen
1905–1977

year: 1943
materials: Beech
prod. by: Fritz Hansen
inv. no.: 196/2005

Søren Hansen was Fritz Hansen's grandson, and he later took over the factory with his brother Fritz. He designed several items of furniture in bent plywood for the factory. The back of the shell chair was bent plywood, attached to a steam-bent frame. The chair was a further development of the factory's DAN chairs (see page 87), a series of steam-bent chairs that Fritz Hansen produced in the 1930s, somewhat similar to the famous Gebrüder Thonet chairs. The shape of the back would serve as inspiration for the seat of Hvidt & Mølgaard's Portex Chair (see page 236) and the back of Jacobsen's Series 7 Chair (see page 254).

3107, the Series 7 Chair

Arne Jacobsen
1902–1971

year: 1955
materials: Plywood, steel tube
prod. by: Fritz Hansen
inv. no.: 7/2009

Moulding plywood for industrial mass production was a key focus area for Fritz Hansen Eftf. They had gained extensive experience from working on Søren Hansen's furniture, Hvidt & Mølgaard's AX, Kjærholm's PK0 and Jacobsen's other shell chairs. Jacobsen designed the Series 7 Chair for Rødovre Town Hall. It was available in a swivel version with armrests and, later, in a range of colours. It is Denmark's bestselling chair and probably the most widely known too, undoubtedly due to its widespread presence in public spaces, including schools, canteens and doctors' waiting rooms.

Production of Series 7 (see page 254)
and other shell chairs at Fritz Hansen.

Arne Jacobsen's Ant Chair (see page 258) in the canteen at Novo, 1950s.

Shell chairs | **3100, the Ant** — Arne Jacobsen

3100, the Ant

Arne Jacobsen
1902–1971

year: 1952
materials: Plywood, steel tube
prod. by: Fritz Hansen
inv. no.: 5/1955

The Ant was the first industrially mass-produced wooden chair with a seat and back in one piece. It was designed for the Danish pharmaceutical company Novo's canteen and quickly became an icon. The Ant was the only chair in the series that did not acquire add-ons such as armrests or padding. The only variation was the four-legged frame, the 3101. Jacobsen insisted on producing the chair with three legs, partly for aesthetic reasons and partly because he believed that a three-legged chair is more stable on an uneven surface. Nevertheless, the four-legged version was the most popular. There was some doubt whether the small, light, three-legged chair would be strong enough, but the Ant and several other chairs in the series have now been in production for more than 50 years.

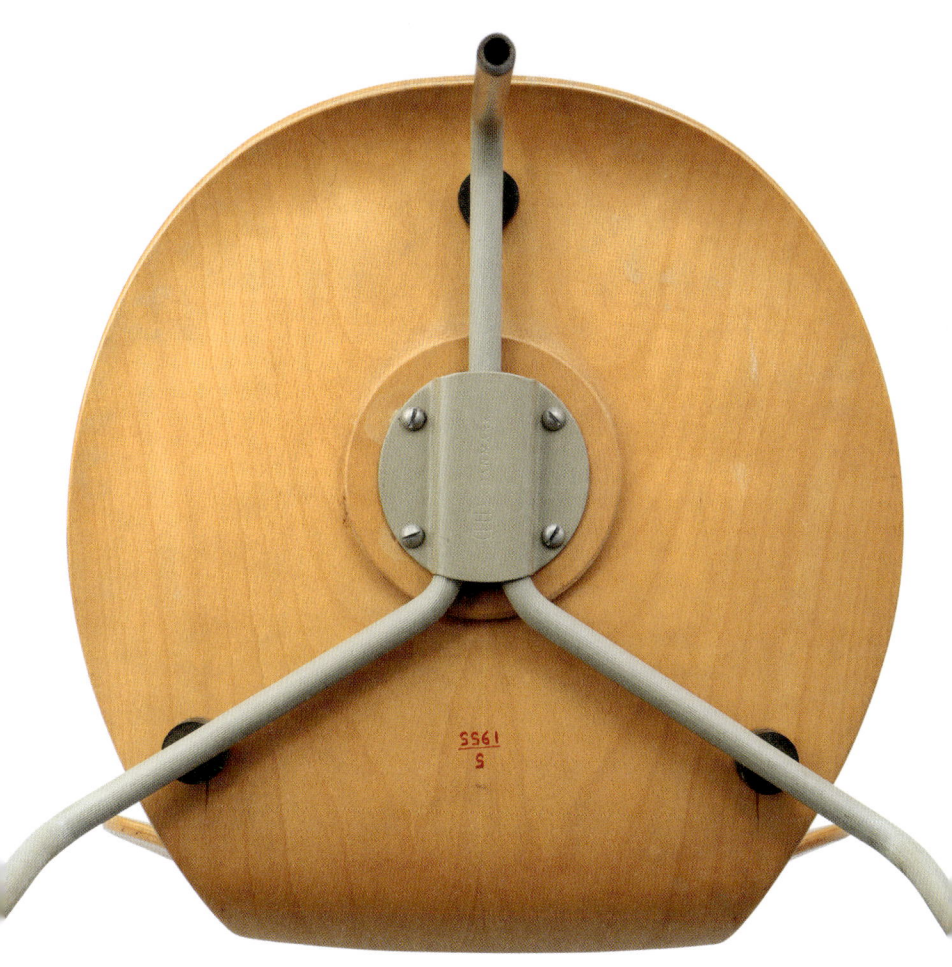

3105, the Mosquito

Arne Jacobsen
1902–1971

year: 1955
materials: Plywood, steel tube
prod. by: Fritz Hansen
inv. no.: 196a/2015

The Mosquito was designed as part of Arne Jacobsen's total design of the Munkegaard School. The chairs and matching tables were designed in three sizes to suit the various age groups. Jacobsen's chairs were initially given a four-digit production number. Later, the public assigned them their various, symbolic nicknames. This one was dubbed the School Chair or the Mosquito. All the chairs in the series consisted of multiple thin layers of beech plywood and cheesecloth with various kinds of face veneers glued together at high temperature and exposed to several tons of pressure.

Production hall at Fritz Hansen with
Arne Jacobsen's Series 7, among other chairs.

Arne Jacobsen's Tongue Chair
(see page 265) used as a classroom
chair at the Munkegaardsskolen
(Munkegaard School).

Shell chairs | **3102, the Tongue** — Arne Jacobsen

3102, the Tongue

Arne Jacobsen
1902–1971

year: 1955
materials: Plywood, steel tube
prod. by: Fritz Hansen
inv. no.: 53/1998

In many ways, 3102, nicknamed the Tongue or the Tie, differs from the other chairs in Jacobsen's series. His simplest chair, it was his personal favourite. The seat is very small, and due to the design of the legs, which differed from those on the other chairs, the chair cannot be stacked. Hence, the company adjusted the otherwise very strict chronological numbering, repositioning it as number 2 in the series. It was intended as a teacher's chair at the Munkegaard School, but was not produced for very long, although production was briefly resumed on several occasions.

4130, Grand Prix

Arne Jacobsen
1902–1971

year: 1957
materials: Plywood, beech
prod. by: Fritz Hansen
inv. no.: 535/2008

This is the only chair in the Jacobsen range with wooden legs. It was launched at the 1957 Danish Crafts Autumn Exhibition at Designmuseum Danmark and, later the same year, was awarded the highest prize at the Milan XI Triennale. Hence, it was dubbed the Grand Prix, just as Kay Bojesen's cutlery was in 1951. The wooden legs meant that the chair could fit in with other traditional cabinetmaker's furnishings. The chair was later produced with tubular-steel legs and was relaunched in 2016 with wooden legs.

Arne Jacobsen's Grand Prix (see page 266),
designed for Fritz Hansen, 1957.

The production hall at Fritz Hansen with Arne Jacobsen's 3103 (see page 270), Mosquito (see page 260) and Series 7 (see page 254).

3103

Arne Jacobsen
1902–1971

year: 1957
materials: Plywood, steel tube
prod. by: Fritz Hansen
inv. no.: 441/2008

3103 is also known as the Orthopaedic Chair and is probably the least known of the series. Professor Egill Snorreson, the leading ergonomics expert of the day, was consulted to help improve the lumbar support that critics said was lacking in Jacobsen's shell chairs. Its somewhat angular back really was more comfortable and was widely used in waiting rooms. There was also a version for children: 3103. Three of the model's 'siblings' also come in children's size: 3105, 3108 and 3107.

3208, the Seagull

Arne Jacobsen
1902–1971

year: 1970
materials: Plywood, wool, steel tube
prod. by: Fritz Hansen
inv. no.: 244/1989

The 3208 Chair is best known with arms, which is why it is referred to either as the Seagull or the Lily. It is the last chair of the six in the series and was designed as part of Jacobsen's total design of Denmark's national bank, the Danmarks Nationalbank. The chair's organic expression was a vivid contrast to Jacobsen's orthogonal architecture. The Seagull has the most curvaceous shell of all Jacobsen's chairs. It was only produced for a short period, because it was pushing the moulding technique to its utmost limits. This led to far too many cracks in the face veneer, so it had to be discontinued.

Arne Jacobsen's Seagull (see page 273) in the boardroom for the Board of Directiors at Danmarks Nationalbank (Denmark's national bank).

Drawing of the Bow Chair
by Grete Jalk (see page 276).

Grete Jalk with the Bow Chair
(see page 276) in her own home.

Shell chairs | **The Bow Chair** – Grete Jalk

The Bow Chair

Grete Jalk
1920–2006

year: 1963
materials: Plywood
prod. by: P. Jeppesens Møbelfabrik
inv. no.: 187/1987

Grethe Jalk created cabinetmaker's furniture, industrial furniture and industrial design. The bow-shaped chair is the technical pinnacle in the evolution of laminated, moulded plywood furniture. The bow curves on one dimension, but the two composite parts make the stool appear to be stretched to a maximum. The structure plays on the vision of a chair in one piece, despite its two-part structure.
To accompany the chair, Jalk designed a set of nesting tables that reiterate the curvature of the seat.

The two-part shell chair, prototype

Hans J. Wegner
1914–2007

year: 1963
materials: Wood, wool
prod. by: Johannes Hansen Møbelsnedkeri
inv. no.: 453/2007

Hans J. Wegner experimented with moulded wooden shells in much of his furniture. The shells appear to hover on the three-legged frame, and the chair comes across more like a sculpture or a form reminiscent of an insect or an animal than as a piece of furniture. This prototype is from 1963. The public had to wait until 1998 before the furniture manufacturer Carl Hansen & Søn put it into production. The prototype has a simpler, but also a less stable leg structure than the model that is currently on the market.

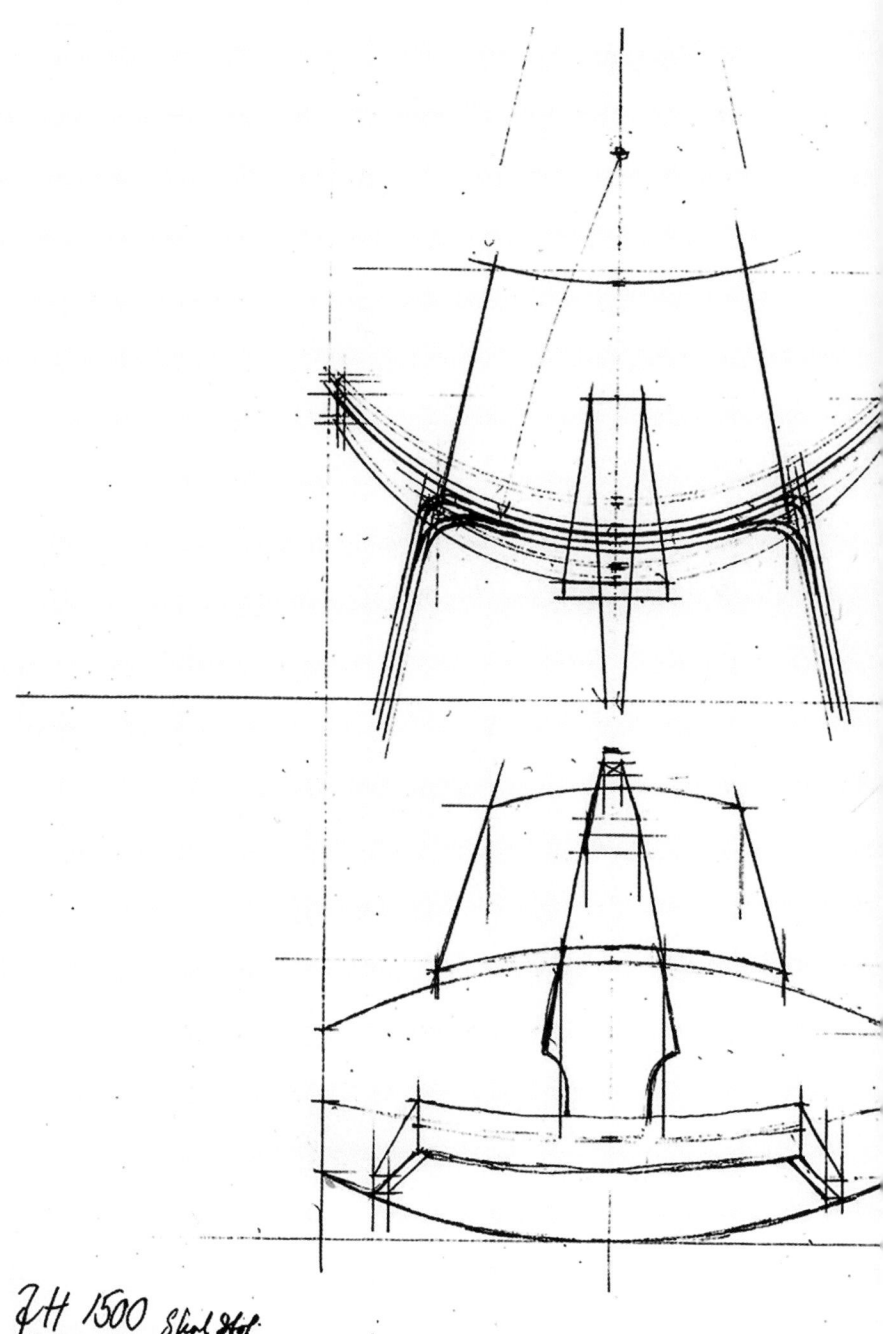

Hans J. Wegner's sketch for the
two-part shell chair (see page 279).

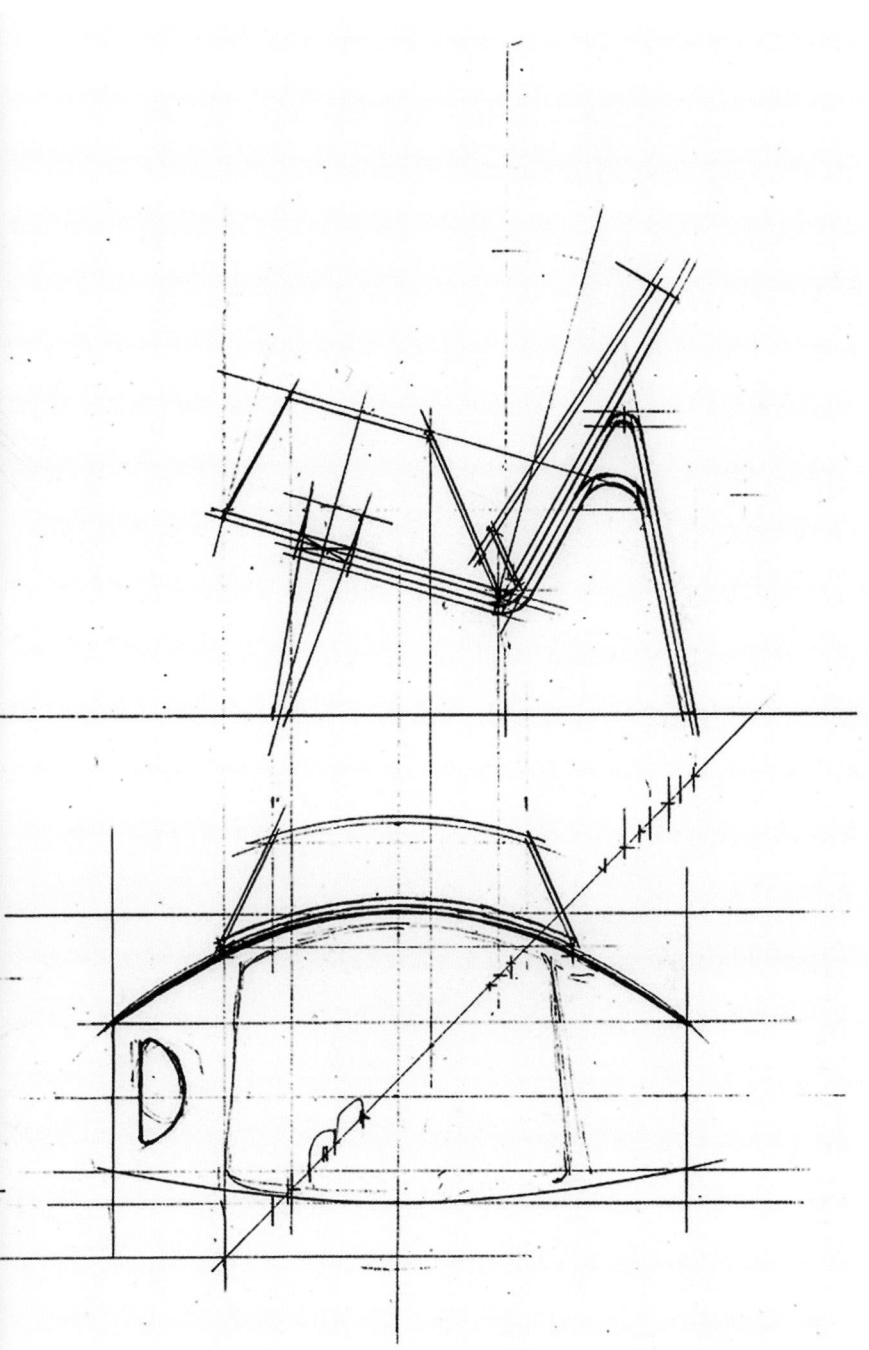

NXT

Peter Karpf
1940-

year: 2001
materials: Beech
prod. by: Iform
inv. no.: 211/2001

Peter Karpf began his training as a cabinetmaker at Fritz Hansen in the 1950s and later became a furniture designer. His interest in shaping plywood resulted in a range of furniture. His first chair was NXT, a stacking chair in one piece. Karpf has subsequently designed several other shaped beech-wood chairs and stools, which form the VOXIA family. With its thin, 3D surfaces, the furniture is designed to ensure minimal wastage of materials.

Trinidad

Nanna Ditzel
1923–2005

year: 1993
materials: Plywood, steel tube
prod. by: Fredericia Furniture
inv. no.: 213b/1994

Nanna Ditzel trained as a cabinetmaker and architect. She is also known for her jewellery and her experimental, decorative approach to design. She drew inspiration from new techniques and production methods. For example, Ditzel used the first CNC (computerised numerically controlled) milling machine in Denmark to cut the characteristic thin slits into the seat and back of the Trinidad Chair. The design was inspired by the fretsaw work on colonial buildings on the Caribbean Islands, and it was originally designed with wooden legs. Ditzel's design of Trinidad marked a new Danish breakthrough for moulded wood. The chair is stackable and is available with seat upholstery and arms.

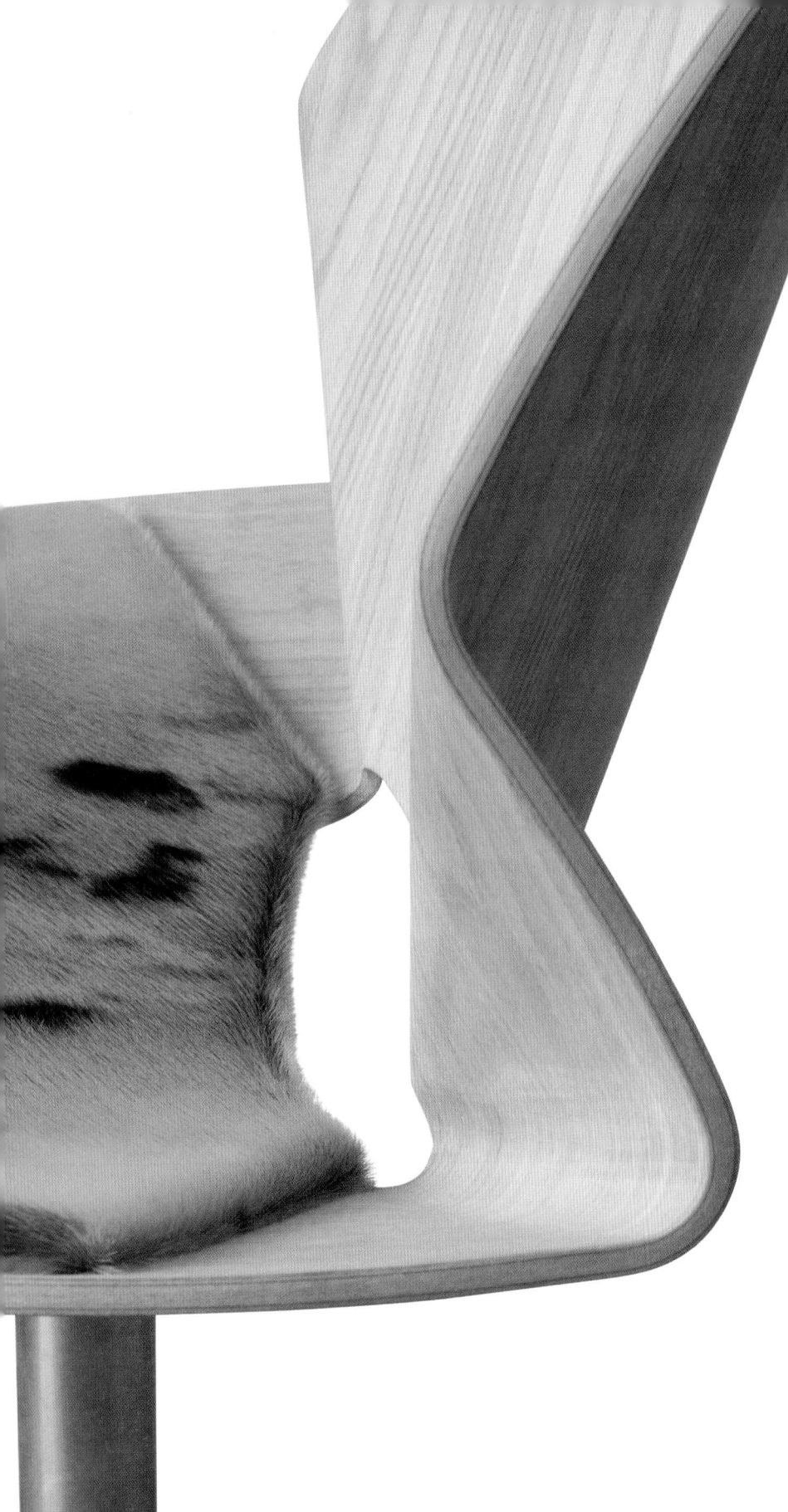

Rex

Christina Strand
1968-

year: 2002
materials: Plywood, sealskin, steel
prod. by: Fredericia Furniture
inv. no.: 324/2004

The designer Christina Strand created the winning chair in the design competition A Chair for the Crown Prince organised by the Danish Crafts and Design Association in 2001. Rex is made of moulded oak plywood with sealskin upholstery as a reference to the Crown Prince's relationship with the nature of the Arctic. The chair's unusual shape was made possible by a combination of folds and a vertical slit where the seat meets the back. The X shape of the undercarriage symbolises the future place of the Crown Prince in the Danish royal lineage as King Frederik X.

Christina Strand's paper folding experiments for the Rex Chair (see page 287).

Boris Berlin and Poul Christiansen's
sketch for the Gubi Chair (see page 290).

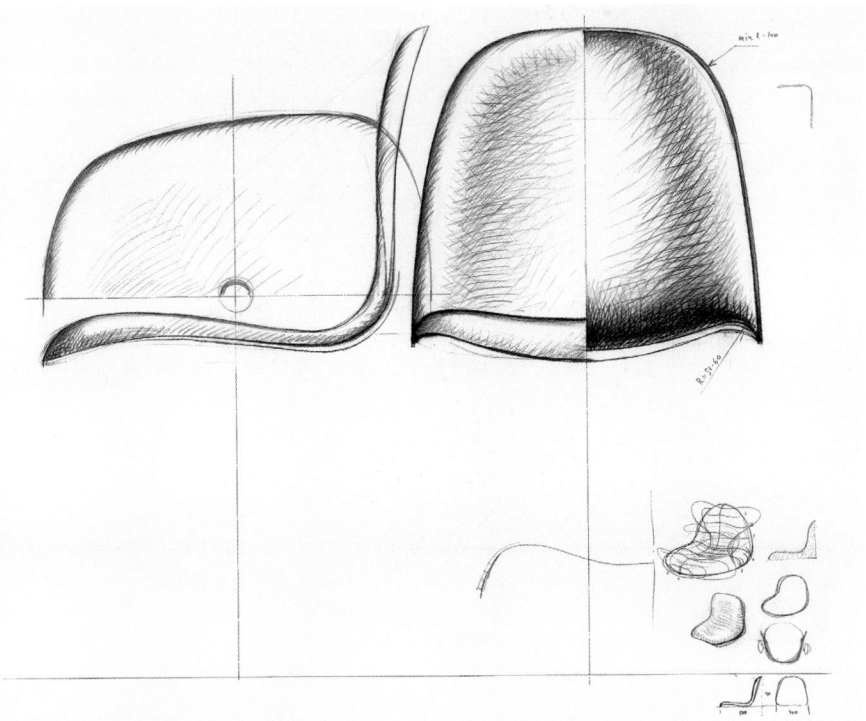

Gubi

Komplot Design

Boris Berlin
1953-
—
Poul Christiansen
1947-

year:	2003
materials:	Plywood, steel
prod. by:	Gubi A/S
inv. no.:	397/2004

The seat and back of the Gubi Chair are made of a single double-curved piece of plywood. The organic 3D shape with curved edges makes the shell stable, ergonomic and open. Designers Berlin and Christiansen used an innovative moulding technique invented in the former German Democratic Republic by Dr Archim Möller. The Gubi Chair was the first industrial application of the technique, which makes the shell only 5 mm thick: approximately half the thickness of traditional shell chairs. The Gubi Chair was named after the manufacturer, whose name was originally inspired by the guppy fish.

Cantilever chairs

The chair without back legs is commonplace today, but the cantilever chair is the only type that does not have pre-industrial roots; indeed, it is the most truly industrial chair, as it would be inconceivable without modern technology. It is a true child of international modernism and a genuine design breakthrough in the history of furniture design.

    The Dutch designer Mart Stam was the first to present a cantilever chair assembled with muffs, in 1926, and soon the type was made in bent seamless steel tubes by several of the great modernists. The goal was a floating seat that did not present an obstacle to the gaze sweeping through open spaces of modernist architecture. However, it also pursued an industrial goal: a chair made of a minimal number of components in order to simplify the manufacturing process. Tubular-steel furniture never became that successful in Denmark, where the main emphasis was on craftsmanship and historical types.

    The tubular-steel cantilever chair was followed by the first cantilever chair in plastic, designed by Danish Verner Panton in 1960: the world's first chair made in a single sheet of plastic. No joints, no components, just a single shell – a cantilever form, as simple and modern as possible, a new chair type for a new time.

294	B64, Cesca, Marcel Breuer
296	6107, Fritz Hansen
298	The Snake Chair, Poul Henningsen
300	Cantilever chair, Torben Skov
302	Weissenhof MR20, Ludwig Mies van der Rohe
304	Cantilever chair, Mogens Lassen
306	EKC20, Poul Kjærholm
308	The Zig-Zag Chair, Gerrit Rietveld
310	Prototype, Poul Kjærholm
314	The S Chair, Verner Panton
318	The Panton Chair, Verner Panton
320	No. 31, Alvar Aalto
322	Cantilever chair, Rud Thygesen & Johnny Sørensen

B64, Cesca

Marcel Breuer (HU)
1902–1981

year: 1928
materials: Steel tube, wickerwork, wood
prod. by: Gebrüder Thonet
inv. no.: 7/1988

In 1925, Marcel Breuer had designed the first domestic tubular-steel chair: B3/Wassily. At the Bauhaus school, where he had been a student and was later to teach, they said, 'eventually we will be sitting on a springy column of air.' Their ideal was an invisible chair that presented no obstacle to the gaze sweeping through the open spatial sequences of the new architecture and further, through huge glass doors, into the landscape. In 1928 came the world's very first chair without back legs: the cantilever chair. Following on the heels of the Dutch designer Mart Stam's version, Breuer's B64 borrowed the bentwood frame and wickerwork of earlier chairs, which perhaps made the chair appear less provocatively modern than it actually was.

6107

Fritz Hansen

year:	ca. 1934
materials:	Steel tube, wickerwork, wood
prod. by:	Fritz Hansen
inv. no.:	94/2010

Fritz Hansen was one of the few Danish companies that tried to sell tubular-steel furniture in Denmark during the 1930s. This chair was clearly inspired by Marcel Breuer's B64 (see page 295). Danes were not crazy about this 'dentist surgery'-style furniture. A cartoon by the Danish illustrator Storm P. depicts two people sitting in tubular-steel furniture. One of them says to the other, 'It doesn't get really comfortable until you run hot water through the pipes.' None of the few Danish tubular-steel furniture designs ever took off in Denmark, as it clashed with the strong tradition for cosy living – 'hygge' – and exquisite cabinetmaker's craftsmanship.

Poul Henningsen with his Snake Chair.

The Snake Chair

Poul Henningsen
1894–1967

year:	1932
materials:	Steel tube, leather
prod. by:	V.A. Høffding
inv. no.:	81/1978

Poul Henningsen was one of the few Danish architects to cultivate international modernism and to sympathise with the likes of the German Bauhaus school. With his Snake Chair, Poul Henningsen attempted to surpass the familiar two-legged cantilever chairs by Mart Stam and Marcel Breuer, among others. A single steel tube, twisted into a coil, constitutes the entire structure of the chair, which in principle has only one leg. As we can see in the chair that is in the collection of Designmuseum Danmark, Henningsen was more preoccupied with the conceptual and expressive qualities of the chair than with whether a single steel tube could actually support someone sitting on it.

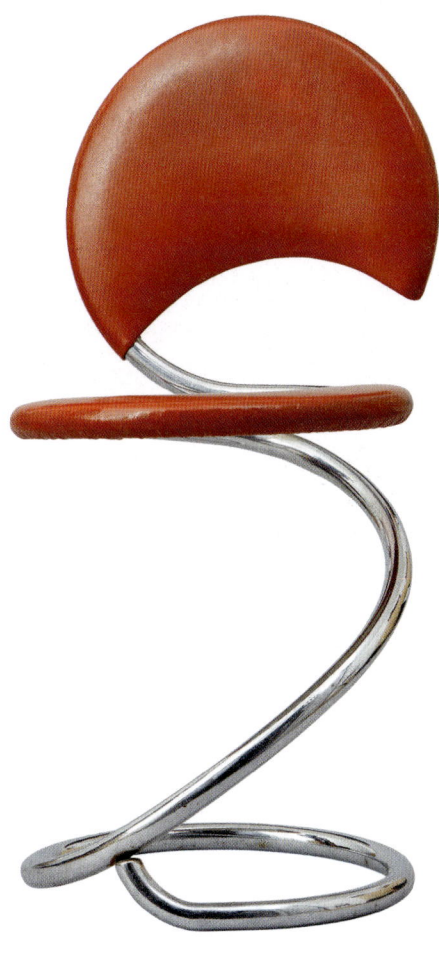

Cantilever chair

Torben Skov
1947-

year: 1988
materials: Steel tubes, plywood
prod. by: Fritz Hansen
inv. no.: 255/1990

The graphic artist and furniture designer Torben Skov is famous for his minimalist, geometrically oriented approach to design. His one-legged chair was presented at the Cabinetmakers' Autumn Exhibition in 1988. Much of Skov's furniture is a continuation of furniture in the Bauhaus tradition. In this chair, he has simplified the cantilever type and the spring effect of bent steel. Unlike most cantilever chairs, this one is stackable.

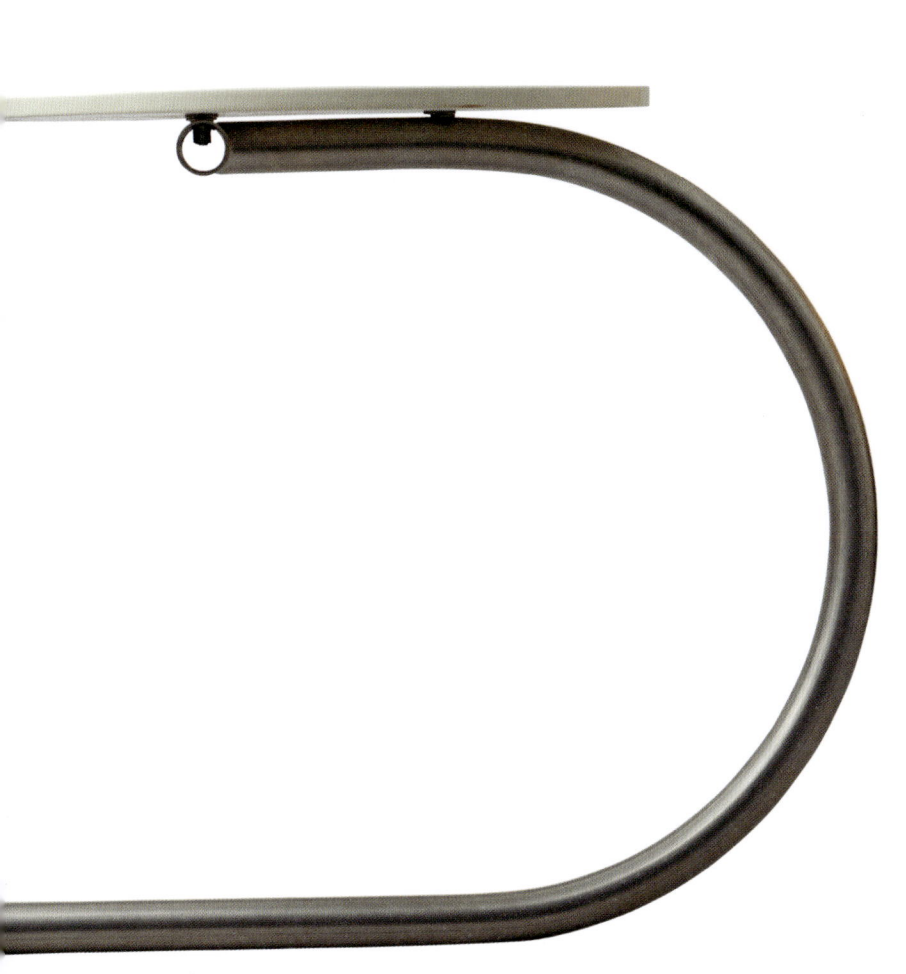

Weissenhof MR20

Ludwig Mies van der Rohe (DE)
1886–1969

year: 1927
materials: Metal, wickerwork
prod. by: Gebrüder Thonet
inv. no.: A129/1933

Ludvig Mies van der Rohe's is a more aesthetic version of a cantilever chair than those by Mart Stam and Marcel Breuer (see page 295). The circle section that constitutes the chair's 'legs' adds to the chair's springy movement, when one sits in it. MR20 was the only tubular-steel chair acquired by Designmuseum Danmark before the 1980s. Professor of Furniture Kaare Klint's traditional view of furniture and outstanding Danish cabinetmaker's craftsmanship shaped the museum's collection policy during the 20th century. The MR20 was the only modernist chair to be included by Ole Wanscher in his major work on the history of furniture making, Møbeltyper (1932). Nonetheless, it did prompt the museum to document the fact that something new was happening on the furniture front in Germany.

Cantilever chair

Mogens Lassen
1901–1987

year: 1933
materials: Steel tube, cane
prod. by: Fritz Hansen
inv. no.: 184/1988

Mogens Lassen was one of the few Danish architects who cultivated international modernism to the full. He had worked for Le Corbusier in France and designed concrete single-family houses north of Copenhagen. His cantilever chair contains clear references to Mies van der Rohe's wicker cantilevers. However, like the more conservative Danish furniture designers, he also looked to history: the form of the chair drew inspiration from a Roman chariot.

EKC20

Poul Kjærholm
1929–1980

year:	1967
materials:	Flat steel, oxhide
prod. by:	E. Kold Christensen
inv. no.:	156/1985

Poul Kjærholm originally trained as a cabinetmaker but worked mainly in steel, like international modernists such as Mies van der Rohe, who also made a springy cantilever chair in flat steel. Kjærholm believed that steel could achieve the same sensuous quality as, say, wood, and age gracefully. To that end, he conducted in-depth studies of various matt chromium-plating techniques. His goal was not to give the steel a cool, industrial expression. Kjærholm was also intrigued by the idea of making furniture that could be disassembled, so it was easy to transport, and in EKC20 the upholstery was sewn using scraps of leather to make the chair sustainable.

The Zig-Zag Chair

Gerrit Rietveld (NL)
1888–1964

year: 1932–1933
materials: Wood
prod. by: Metz & Co.
inv. no.: D1758

Gerrit Rietveld's Zig-Zag Chair is sculptural and simple. Here the focus is on the striking and beautiful construction. Rietveld was a member of the Dutch design group De Stijl, whose proponents favoured abstract and distorted forms. He himself said, 'It isn't a chair but a designer joke.' In other words, this was not about comfort or ergonomics but about pursuing the idea of a chair – an abstraction that challenged the very concept of a chair. A particularly interesting aspect is the illusion that the chair is in one piece, which Verner Panton was later to achieve, and the highlighting of the joints and screws. For the modernists, honest, easily decoded structures were a goal in themselves.

Prototype

Poul Kjærholm
1929–1980

year: 1953
materials: Steel
inv. no.: 36a-c/2001

Poul Kjærholm's prototype rose to the challenge of creating a cantilever chair in a single piece: something most modernists dreamed of. Mies van der Rohe made similar sketches as early as the 1930s. It fell to Verner Panton to realise the idea with his Panton Chair (see page 319), a high dining chair. Kjærholm's prototype was not realised, because he lacked the necessary technology.

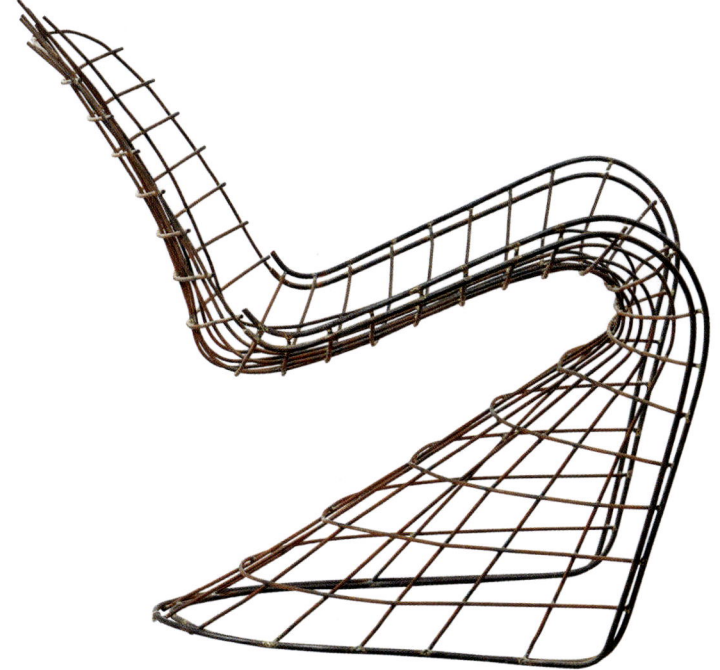

Poul Kjærholm's drawing of
wire prototype (see page 311).

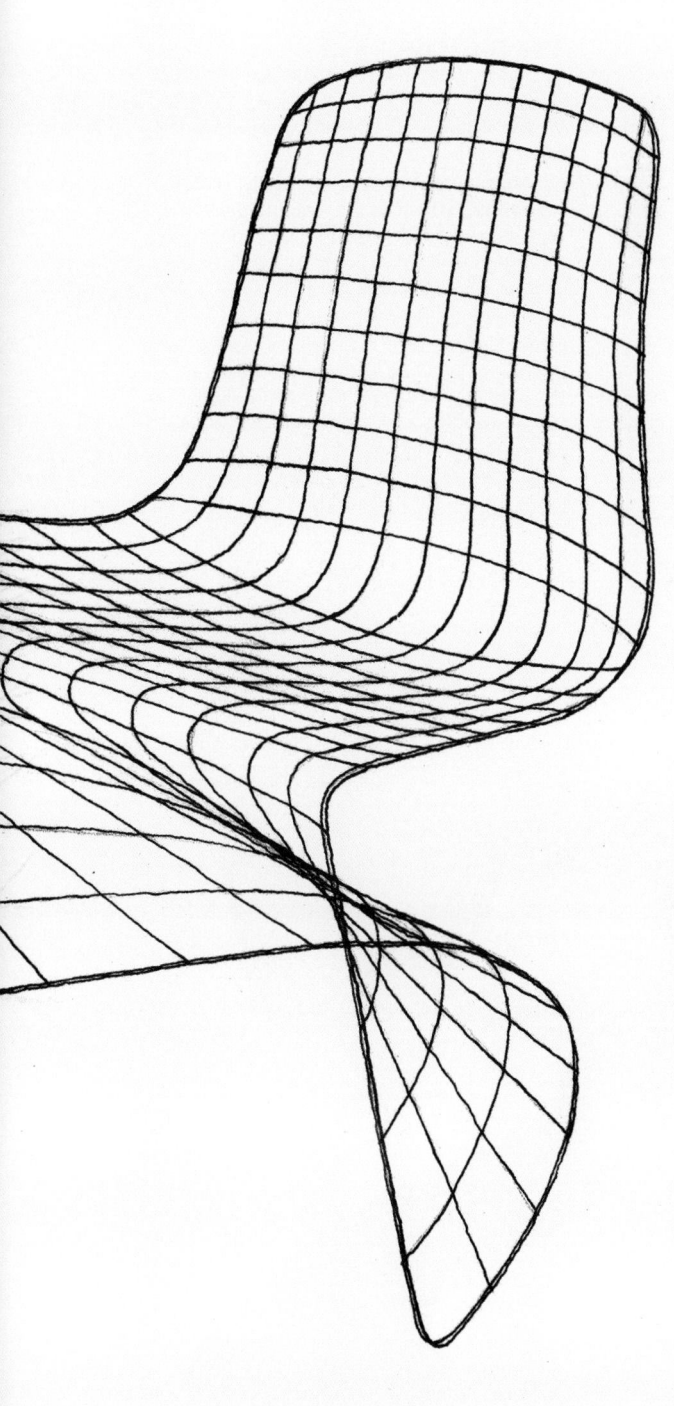

The S Chair

Verner Panton
1926–1998

year: 1956
materials: Plywood
prod. by: Gebrüder Thonet
inv. no.: 173/2001

Verner Panton's S Chair is a cantilever chair: a precursor of what is perhaps his most famous chair, the Panton Chair (see page 319). The S Chair is made of moulded plywood and can be regarded as a continuation of Arne Jacobsen's pursuit of constructive simplification in the Ant (see page 258): a single shell, seat and back in one piece. Panton worked for Arne Jacobsen and was involved in developing the Ant. He designed the S Chair when he opened his own studio. It realises the modernists' dream of a chair without back legs, created in one piece and in a material that made it more industrial.

Hallway space at the office of Der Spiegel decorated by Verner Panton, featuring the S Chair (see page 314).

Panton's daughter Carin with a row of
Panton Chairs, ca. 1968 (see page 319).

Manfred Diebold, Rolf Fehlbaum,
Verner Panton and an employee
in the development department
at Herman Miller/Vitra, ca. 1961.

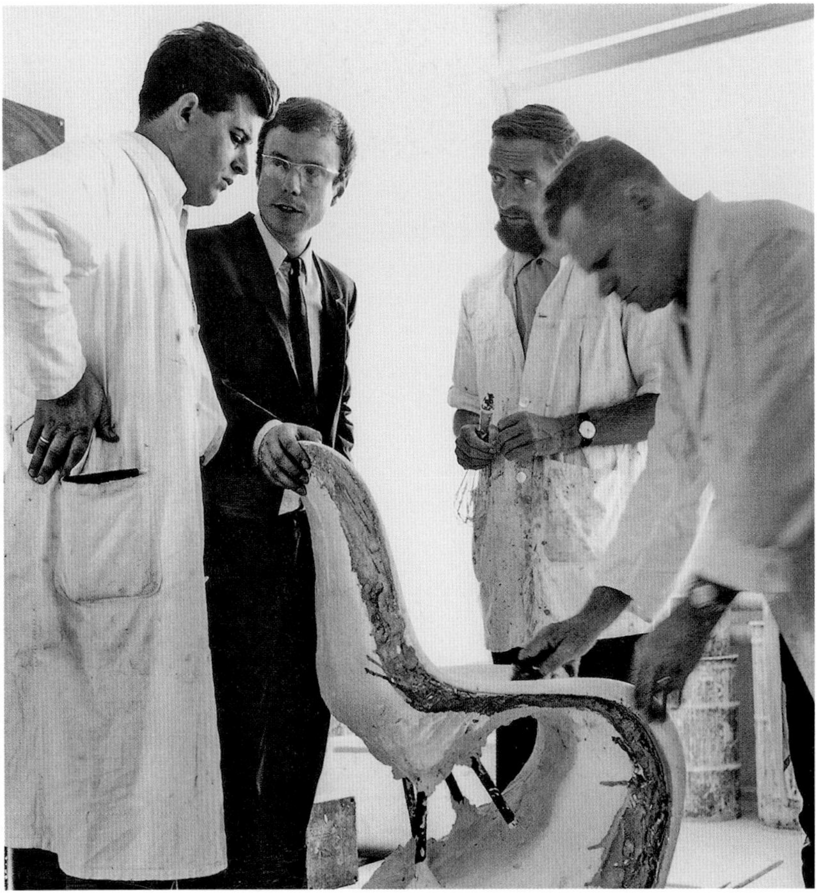

Cantilever chairs | **The Panton Chair** – Verner Panton

The Panton Chair

Verner Panton
1926–1998

year: 1960/1967–1968
materials: Plastic
prod. by: Herman Miller
inv. no.: 116a-b/1985

Verner Panton was the enfant terrible of Danish design, departing radically from the Danish design tradition, which was based on craftsmanship, wood and muted colours. The famous plastic stacking chair was the world's first-ever mass-produced chair with legs, seat and back made of a single piece of plastic. A chair without back legs: a cantilever chair. Panton loved colours and believed that 'you sit more comfortably in a colour you like.' The brightly coloured chair reflected the new consumer culture of the time, the playful pop age culture and a departure from the cabinetmaking tradition.

Cantilever chairs | **The Panton Chair** – Verner Panton

No. 31

Alvar Aalto (FI)
1898–1976

year: 1931–1932
materials: Plywood, birch
inv. no.: 22/1991

Alvar Aalto was one of the greatest Scandinavian architects of the 20th century. His introduction of laminated wood combined with an international, modernist idiom made him one of the pioneers of Scandinavian organic modernism. He made this chair for the Paimio Sanitarium, which Aalto designed in its entirety in 1928–32, along with the Paimio Chair – another iconic Aalto chair. In this chair, Aalto proved it was possible to make a chair without back legs with a springy effect comparable to that of the German tubular steel cantilever chairs. Consequently, the chair acquired a more human, warmer expression, which was a better match for the Scandinavian lifestyle.

Cantilever chair

Rud Thygesen
1932-2019
—
Johnny Sørensen
1944-

year: 1975
materials: Beech, jute webbing
prod. by: Magnus Olesen
inv. no.: 54/1976

Rud Thygesen and Johnny Sørensen made this chair in 1975 for the Furniture Fair at Designmuseum Danmark. It is a further reworking of the cantilever type, but instead of steel it is made of wood. This was something the Finnish architect and designer, Alvar Aalto had already begun doing back in the 1930s. Thygesen and Sørensen experimented with the sides to distribute the load on the chair. The front brace absorbs the torsion, and the back brace absorbs the pressure. Thygesen and Sørensen's experiments with laminated wood in the 1970s resulted in furniture that was widely used in Denmark's public sector: in hospitals, nursing homes, preschools and so forth.

Danish furniture designers who shaped their field

The furniture designers presented in the following pages all represent and shaped the Danish approach to furniture design and inspired many others.

Kaare Klint, Ole Wanscher, Mogens Koch and Børge Mogensen all wholeheartedly embrace wood and the development of historical furniture types.

Hans J. Wegner and Finn Juhl address historical types but are also inspired by contemporary art and international post-war organic modernism. That matches the spirit of the times in countries outside Denmark, and hence they have their biggest success abroad with Danish Modern in the mid 20th century.

Arne Jacobsen too is an international modernist. He is inspired by contemporary design abroad and he designs some of the first truly industrial chairs in Denmark in an organic idiom. He develops and improves the new furniture types of the 20th century, including the shell chair and the polystyrene chair, and in that sense he too is a proponent of the Danish furniture approach. Poul Kjærholm refines early international modernist furniture types in steel and laminated wood, translating them to a Danish expression and adding a more haptic dimension to international modernism.

Verner Panton challenges virtually all aspects of Danish design. He uses synthetic materials and works with room installations and pop design, but he also takes on the chair types of international modernism, rethinking the cantilever chair – the chair without back legs – and the concept of the chair in a single piece.

326 —— Kaare Jensen Klint
327 —— Mogens Koch
328 —— Ole Wanscher
329 —— Børge Vestergaard Mogensen
330 —— Hans Jørgensen Wegner
331 —— Finn Juhl
332 —— Arne Emil Jacobsen
333 —— Poul Kjærholm
334 —— Verner Panton

Kaare Jensen Klint
1888–1954

The architect Kaare Klint's training included Technical College, an apprenticeship as a house painter and studies under the painter and furniture designer Johan Rohde at Kunstnernes Frie Studieskoler (The Artists' Free Study Schools). He also took lessons from his own father, P. V. Jensen Klint, the architect of Grundtvig's Church. During the 1910s Klint developed a fascination with the return of neoclassicism. From the architect Carl Petersen he learned to appreciate the Danish tradition of classic realism, as exemplified by C. F. Harsdorff, N. A. Abildgaard, M. G. Bindesbøll and H. E. Freund.

Carl Petersen included the proportions of the human body as a factor in his work because he understood their impact on the way we experience architecture. Klint similarly studied human proportions and movements in order to give his furniture proper and functional dimensions. It was important to strike the right relationship between anatomy and furniture measurements, just as furniture had to be proportioned for the room it was intended for.

In 1923 a new school of furniture was established at the Royal Danish Academy of Fine Arts, and Klint was employed as a teacher. In 1924 he made associate professor, and in 1944 he was appointed as professor. Both as a furniture designer and as a teacher Klint came to influence an entire generation of Danish furniture designers. Several world-renowned Danish furniture designers came from what became known as the Klint School.

Kaare Klint was not influenced by the international functionalism that reached Scandinavia in the late 1920s. He rejected the attempts of Bauhaus to jettison tradition and start over from scratch on a purely analytical basis. However, although Klint believed the right approach was to build on the experience handed down through tradition, his teaching and his own furniture had more than a little in common with international functionalism and its ideas about standardisation and rationalisation. Klint required his students to include social concerns in their work, and his teaching always had an analytical perspective. The students acquired in-depth knowledge of genuine materials and strong constructions, in part through studying historical furniture.

Klint's own furniture proves that functional analysis is compatible with the reinterpretation of historical furniture (including furniture from antiquity, Chippendale chairs and Shaker furniture). Provided they were properly proportioned, and the materials were well chosen, historical models could easily be reused. External stylistic features and a personal expression were less important. Klint rejected the stylistic copying of 19th-century furniture and considered *skønvirke* (Danish art nouveau) furniture impractical and domineering in scale and expression. Although Klint may be regarded an aristocratic furniture designer, and the costly materials and exacting craftsmanship required to make his furniture placed it beyond the reach of ordinary buyers, his ideas about typological categories and standard measurements anticipated the more affordable industrial Danish everyday furniture.

Mogens Koch
1898–1992

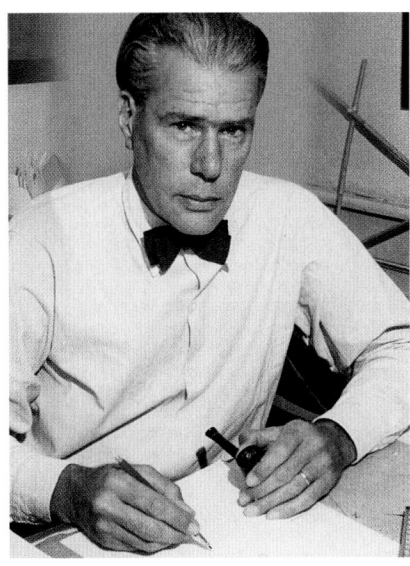

Mogens Koch trained as a building architect at the Royal Danish Academy of Fine Arts, School of Architecture, but he must be considered a generalist, having worked with most domains of architecture and design, including city planning, buildings, monuments, furniture, textile, silver, typeface and exhibition planning. In his youth he worked with the architects Carl Petersen, Ivar Bentsen, Kaare Klint, Povl Baumann and Ole Falkentorp. In 1934 he founded his own studio. Like Kaare Klint, Koch introduced building restoration as a new discipline at the Academy and was appointed as professor of this field in 1950. For a number of years he worked mainly with the restoration of both churches and secular buildings.

Koch had attended Kaare Klint's Furniture School, and while working with Kaare Klint he had been involved in the conversion of the former hospital Frederiks Hospital to Designmuseum Danmark. As a designer, Koch always prioritised the whole above the detail, and like Klint he strove for harmony between building, furniture and other interior design items. As a restoration architect he was also no stranger to the idea of building on the experiences of previous generations of architects.

The few but carefully analysed and unembellished pieces of furniture that Koch designed were all created for a specific purpose or building. Koch created his most famous furniture design, the square bookcase, for his own home, one of the architect Povl Baumann's small terraced houses in the Hulgaarden settlement, as early as 1928. It meets all Klint's requirements for functional furniture design: it is flexible, compact and divided into sections matching contemporary book formats.

Like Klint, Koch also worked with numbers and geometry, both in his historical studies and in his efforts to achieve harmonious proportions in furniture and other designs. Despite his work with standardised modules Koch, like Klint and Ole Wanscher, had few industrial assignments. Koch's practical, straightforward and anonymous furniture is made of hard-wearing, maintenance-free materials, as prescribed by the Danish cabinetmaking tradition. Koch is one of the clearest proponents of the functionalist ideals of the Klint School.

Ole Wanscher
1903–1985

Ole Wanscher was the son of the art historian Vilhelm Wanscher, who is known for the book *Architekturens Historie* (History of Architecture) 1931. Ole Wanscher graduated from the School of Building Technology in 1924 before continuing his studies at the Royal Danish Academy of Fine Arts, School of Architecture in Copenhagen. In 1925–1927 he was an employee at Kaare Klint's design firm. In 1927 he founded his own studio, specialising in furniture design, and he was also a prolific writer, especially on the topic of furniture design. In 1931–1936 he taught furniture design at the School Arts and Crafts. In 1955 Wanscher's principal work, *Møbelkunsten – Studier i Møbeltypernes Æstetik og Historie* (Furniture Design – Studies in the Aesthetic and History of Furniture Types) was published, the same year as he succeeded Kaare Klint as Professor of Furniture Design at the Academy. Wanscher's interest and reuse of historical furniture in his own furniture design made him an obvious choice for the position. In his studies of furniture design history Wanscher's focus was not purely stylistic but also included materials and constructions as conditions for the development of the various furniture types.

Wanscher's earliest designs were clearly influenced by Kaare Klint, but while Klint mainly worked with tradition in a desire to find support for his own works, Wanscher, influenced by his father, wanted to paint a broader picture of furniture design, decoding it as a manifestation of formal concepts of earlier cultures without imposing his own assessment.

His own furniture was modelled mainly on English furniture from the 18th century and on Egyptian furniture types. Wanscher did not share Klint's interest in the standardisation of furniture dimensions based on functional concerns, a fascination with mathematical systems and the desire to achieve a precise, easily recognisable form based on geometry. Wanscher's interest lay more with comfortable seating and free-flowing lines adapted to the human body. His interest in aesthetic and, in particular, constructive issues led him continuously to refine the details of his many seating furniture designs. In his work with basic furniture forms, which were often inspired by historical styles, he strove for a more delicate, lighter and more elegant expression.

Wanscher also did not share Klint's interest in anonymous traditional furniture. Instead, his furniture was influenced by the aristocratic and exclusive qualities of bourgeois furniture design, with mahogany and rosewood as his preferred woods. Although Wanscher did take an interest in the social ideas that were represented in the modernism of the International Style in the early 1930s, he saw no connection between the tubular-steel furniture and the endorsed ideals. Most of his furniture types remained finely crafted cabinetmaker's furniture. Some of his designs were later adapted to small-scale industrial production.

Børge Vestergaard Mogensen
1914–1972

Børge Mogensen completed his cabinet-maker's apprenticeship in 1934 in his native city of Ålborg on the Limfjord strait. The local area remained a fundamental influence throughout his life, and in his later years he spent much of his time here. In 1936–1938 he attended the School of Arts and Crafts in Copenhagen at the same time as Hans J. Wegner. In contrast to predecessors such as Kaare Klint, Ole Wanscher and Mogens Koch, who came from Copenhagen's upper middle class, both Mogensen and Wegner came from a modest background outside the capital region. They were also the first to be able to make a living exclusively as furniture designers. Mogensen went on to attend Kaare Klint's Furniture School at the Royal Danish Academy of Fine Arts from 1938 to 1942. He worked at both Mogens Koch's and Kaare Klint's firms. In 1945–1947 he worked as an assistant to Klint at the Furniture School. He was Klint's successor in only one official position, that of architect for Designmuseum Danmark after Klint's death in 1954.

Few Danish architects have so clearly understood and continued Klint's rational approach as Mogensen did, with his grasp of systematics and visualised order. Where the previous generation of furniture designers failed in their striving for standardisation, Mogens succeeded. Mogensen carried the craft-based ideals into the industrial context. Serially produced furniture sold in furniture shops is his principal contribution to the history of furniture design, although he also designed furnishings for large interior design assignments and was active as an exhibition architect. In the design of furnishing fabrics he made a large contribution through his long-standing cooperation with weaver Lis Ahlmann.

In his factory-made furniture Mogensen combined the Klint School's constructive and aesthetic ideals with the social consciousness that emerged within applied arts after the breakthrough of functionalism.

The purpose of the Fællesforeningen for Danmarks Brugsforeninger (The Confederation of Danish Manufacturing and Retail Cooperatives, FDB) was to provide the members with a full range of high-quality everyday products at the lowest possible price. FDB commissioned architect, Professor Steen Eiler Rasmussen to define a conceptual framework for the industrial production of furniture. He arranged the appointment of Børge Mogensen as head of FDB's furniture design studio in 1942, a position Mogensen retained until 1950 when he founded his own design studio in Frederiksberg near Copenhagen. FDB aimed to create furniture that met the practical needs of an average family.

Mogensen applied Klint's analytical 'research method' to test his model in his 'housing lab', two model homes, one for a working-class family and one for a family in a rural setting. His housing studies were far more extensive than Klint's, but on the rare occasion when it was necessary, he was willing to compromise – something that was unthinkable to Klint or to perfectionists such as Arne Jacobsen and Poul Kjærholm.

The design of storage furniture plays an important role in Mogensen's production. His series of shelving and cabinet elements for FDB, like the modular construction furniture he created for Mogens Koch, could be combined into larger wall units. Like Klint, Mogensen based his design on tableware dimensions, simple mathematical systems and anthropometrically determined heights.

Mogensen was not particularly interested in contemporary international design. Like Klint, he felt that traditional furniture types that had proved their utilitarian worth and durability for centuries could be improved and simplified. English Windsor chairs, Swedish spindle-back chairs and American Shaker chairs were the models of his FDB furniture. Later he also turned to furniture by Klint and Koch.

A trained cabinetmaker, Børge Mogensen preferred working in solid wood, leather and textile. His goal was always total clarity with regard to materials, construction and form. His furniture is not shaped by aesthetic abstractions or imaginative shapes but by practical needs. Like Klint, Mogensen regarded furniture design as a mechanical art, as opposed to a liberal art. Hence, he preferred to design furniture for a specific context – initially FDB's model flats, later his own home by Ermelunden north of Copenhagen, which was renovated repeatedly, and finally Landhuset (the Country House) by the Limfjorden strait.

Hans Jørgensen Wegner
1914–2007

Hans J. Wegner acquired his interest in crafts through his upbringing. His father was a shoemaker. Wegner had a natural talent for working in wood and trained as a carpenter. After a few years of working as a cabinetmaker and studies at the cabinetmaker's course at the Tehcnical College, Wegner attended the School of Arts and Crafts in Copenhagen until 1938. He later taught at the school. In 1939 Wegner worked for the architects Erik Møller and Flemming Lassen, and in 1940–1943 for Arne Jacobsen and Erik Møller. During this time, he designed furniture for Århus City Hall, among other assignments. In 1943–1946 Wegner had his own studio in Århus. In 1946–1948 he worked at Palle Suenson's studio in Copenhagen before once again founding his own studio. During the war years, Wegner also worked with his close friend from the School of Arts and Crafts Børge Mogensen, who headed the FDB's design office. Together, they created a range of good, simple and affordable furniture.

Although Wegner did design two houses (his own home and a summerhouse), a few light fittings and other examples of applied art and designed countless offices, exhibitions and showrooms, it was his work as a chair designer – totalling about 500 different models – that earned him international fame. Like Børge Mogensen, Wegner was one of the first leading Danish furniture designers who trained as a cabinetmaker. Wegner's work represents a lifelong endeavour to understand the nature of materials. Although Wegner's chairs are shaped by the inherent logic of wood, Wegner is not a rational, analytical furniture designer like Børge Mogensen. Wegner approach is always experimental, his goal is not harmonious form, but expressive, intriguing form. If Børge Mogensen as a furniture designer represents 'the scientist', Wegner is 'the artist'.

Wegner pursues and repeatedly returns to certain formal themes in his chairs. Initially, like the Klint students, he revisited historical furniture types, aiming to simplify, improve and resurrect them in their pure construction. Designmuseum Danmark has a number of Chinese chairs from the 18th century, all exquisitely crafted with a box-shaped base and an upper part in a freer form. Wegner took an interest in the chairs when he saw them reproduced in Ole Wanscher's 1932 book Møbeltyper (Furniture Types). Chinese chairs was a theme that had previously been addressed by Wegner's employer Arne Jacobsen in his furniture for the restaurant at the Bellevue Theatre from 1937. Wegner created several reinterpretations of the theme that are quite close to the original. Through simplification, he was gradually able to create a contemporary Danish chair. At the Copenhagen Cabinetmakers' Guild's furniture exhibition in 1949 he presented the Round Chair, which the American magazine Interiors dubbed The Chair the following year. This simultaneously luxurious and spartan handcrafted chair earned Wegner world fame as one of the finest representatives of Danish design. Subsequently, Wegner created numerous chairs with armrests based on the same theme. The organic forms in wood make Wegner a close relative of Finn Juhl's, but he never pushes the wood to extremes, nor does he pursue a strictly sculptural expression. Instead he sometimes draws inspiration from old practical tools, such as axe handles, scythe handles and oar blades – shapes with a strong tactile appeal.

Like Ole Wanscher and Børge Mogensen, among others, Wegner also created several interpretations of the English Windsor chair. However, Wegner not only strives to simplify and clarify the type but always aims for a highly independent expression. In the Peacock Chair, for example, Wegner goes beyond the functionalism that other furniture makers pursued in the Windsor chair. The extravagant, stem-bent back brace lends the chair a grandiose air, akin to the Chinese nobleman's chair in cane with its circular wickerwork back. In a deviation from the work of Klint and several of his students, Wegner does not pursue any ideological ambitions in his reuse and development of historical furniture types. Also, some of Wegner's chairs have no specific historical model.

In technical and constructive terms, Wegner was anything but conservative. Few designers have worked with so many different furniture manufacturers. Wegner's chairs demand a high level of craftsmanship, but he always sought to maximise the use of industrial processes. Several of his early chairs were later modified to facilitate industrial manufacturing.

Wegner also designed furniture in new materials, including steel. In 1948 he took part in the international design competition for low-cost furniture design for the home held by the Museum of Modern Art in New York. Here, contemporaneously with the American designer Charles Eames, he demonstrated that a chair could be made of moulded plywood shells – a theme that Arne Jacobsen addressed a few years later. Although Wegner made excellent shell chairs they play a minor role in his work. In the long run, the cabinetmaker's love of solid wood prevailed.

Finn Juhl
1912–1989

Finn Juhl came from a moneyed Copenhagen upper-middle-class background. Even as a child, he was so interested in art that he would visit the Glyptotek and the SMK, the national gallery of Denmark, and he wanted to be an art historian. His father thought the prospects of the profession too meagre, however, so as a compromise, Finn Juhl enrolled at the Royal Danish Academy of Fine Arts, School of Architecture after graduating from upper secondary school in 1930. He studied with Kay Fisker, while Gunnar Asplund's functionalism was gaining momentum in the Nordic countries. Juhl became a competent all-round building architect, but he never graduated. In 1934–1945 he worked in his teacher Vilhelm Lauritzen's studio, making important contributions to the interior of one of the most important functionalist monuments in Denmark: Radiohuset (the Radio Building). In 1945 Juhl founded his own studio. Among the few buildings he designed was his own house in Ordrup Krat north of Copenhagen, completed in 1942. From his youth, Finn Juhl took part in the debate about the interior design of non-profit housing, among other issues, arguing the need for architects to base their building design on the design of the rooms inside the building. His own architecture was always designed from the inside out, the exterior based on the room and the interior.

Already during his youth, Finn Juhl designed furniture for his own flat and had cabinetmaker Niels Vodder produce them. This led to a collaboration that would last for years. The idea of designing furniture for one's own home is an old tradition going back to the painter Nicolai Abildgaard, the architect M. G. Bindesbøll and the sculptor H. E. Freund – the so-called 'artist's furniture'. Throughout his life, Juhl emphasised that as a furniture-maker he was self-taught, but nevertheless, furniture design was his principal field. He exhibited his first, somewhat heavy, padded furniture at the Copenhagen Cabinetmakers' Guild's furniture exhibition in 1937, where it drew considerable attention. It was a furniture type that was far removed from prevailing ideas at the craft-oriented furniture schools at the Royal Danish Academy of Fine Arts and the School of Arts of Crafts.

Although Juhl's furniture was based on functional analysis, it marked a clear deviation from the Klint School's rational, traditional and geometrically defined furniture. Juhl did not want to base his designs on developments of historical furniture types; instead he wanted to make new designs inspired by contemporary art. His furniture not only resembled sculptures by artists such as Henry Moore, Hans Arp, Barbara Hepworth and Erik Thommesen; he also typically presented it alongside sculptures by these artists. His interior design too was inspired by sculpture, with bodies in free and bound movement.

After a few years, Finn Juhl discovered that overstuffed furniture was not necessarily more comfortable than lightly padded furniture. He therefore began to use thinner padding and aimed for an extreme degree of formal precision. This lent his furniture designs a ligher visual expression. By studying Ole Wanscher's books on the history of furniture design he discovered Egyptian furniture design, which he felt had 'an animalistically satisfying character'. The organic wooden frames in which seats, backrests and armrests were 'suspended', highlighted the relationship between 'the bearing' and 'the borne' – as in Poul Kjærholm's designs, but with a very different expression. The organically shaped components were assembled with invisible and highly unorthodox wooden joints. He pushed the potential of the material to extremes, as Arne Jacobsen did in his furniture. That demanded excellent craftsmanship and made the furniture poorly suited for industrial production. The elegant, supple and delicate shapes required woods and cuts of the highest quality: teak, maple, cherry, Oregon pine, cedar, hickory and rosewood. Juhl was one of the first to use teak for indoor furniture. That played an important role in the popularity of teak furniture during the 1960s.

Although the high-end furniture was expensive, Juhl's designs did go into industrial production, first in the United States and later in Denmark. In the early 1950s, Juhl developed good connections in the US, where he had been commissioned to design the interior of the Trusteeship Council Chamber at the Headquarters of the United Nations in New York. He did a number of interior design commissions in Europe, the US and Asia for SAS, Georg Jensen and Bing & Grøndahl, among others. He also designed many exhibitions of Danish design and applied art abroad.

Arne Emil Jacobsen
1902–1971

The architect Arne Jacobsen had a great talent for drawing and wanted to be a painter, but after completing lower secondary school he enrolled at Polytechnic College and from there he went on to attend the Royal Danish Academy of Fine Arts, School of Architecture in Copenhagen. Here he studied under the architects Ivar Bentsen, Kay Fisker and Kaj Gottlob and graduated in 1927.

From the outset, Jacobsen had an excellent grasp of the prevailing architectural tradition in Denmark. In accordance with his training, he began by designing houses in what Kay Fisker referred to as 'the functional tradition', influenced by N. A. Abildgaard and M. G. Bindesbøll. However, like the Swedish architect Gunnar Asplund, whom Jacobsen admired, he soon deviated from the gracious neoclassical expression and embraced 'the white style' represented by Bauhaus in Germany and Le Corbusier in France.

After the Second World War, Jacobsen contributed to the emergence of a more regional variant of modernism by reintroducing yellow brickwork and designing houses with sloping roofs and freer curves. During the second half of the 1950s Jacobsen was attracted to the modernism that had weathered out the war in the United States, brought in by European immigrants. Minimalists such as Mies van der Rohe, Eliel Saarinen and Skidmore, Owings & Merrill working with steel, glass, aluminium and polished stone had shaped much of the expression that Jacobsen mastered to perfection.

Jacobsen's mastery of details was instrumental in bringing about his international fame. He had not only developed an outstanding grasp of proportions, based on the Danish neoclassical tradition; he also felt that every item in a house should be included in the architectural commission. Several of Jacobsen's major works are total designs or *Gesamtkunstwerke*, total works of art. From day one, Jacobsen was fully aware that our perception of a room depends in part on the decorative and utilitarian items in it. Thus, he designed all the installations, furniture, light fittings, clocks, loudspeaker, sanitation, cutlery, glasses, ashtrays, a wide range of fittings, wallpapers and fabric patterns for several of his large architectural assignments, including the Novo annex from 1952, Rødovre City Hall from 1955, the SAS Royal Hotel from 1959, St. Catherine's College from 1963 and Nationalbanken (Denmark's national bank) from 1970–1972. The items were later put into production for everyday contexts and helped make Jacobsen famous as a world-class industrial designer.

Jacobsen's interest in details was part of his pronounced perfectionism. He held the manufacturers of his design products to extremely high standards. His industrial furniture had to possess a technical quality and finish on level with the best hand-crafted products. The moulded laminated shell chairs were perhaps Jacobsen's greatest innovation, both technically and formally. They mark a watershed and a zenith in the history of Danish furniture design as some of the first examples of industrially manufactured furniture in Denmark.

Jacobsen began to receive international recognition while he was still a student, when he exhibited furniture designed for cabinetmaker Niels Vodder at the 1925 World's Fair in Paris and was awarded a silver medal. Jacobsen's early furniture adhered to the crafts spirit of the Klint School. Although Jacobsen did design furniture pieces with an industrial appearance around 1930, clearly inspired by Bauhaus, he realised that the technology for mass production was not yet ready in Denmark and so continued to furnish his buildings with more conventional hand-crafted furniture. The Ant was a turning point in Jacobsen's design career. Here he abandoned the national furniture and crafts tradition to take on the challenges of industrial production. Almost all Jacobsen's chairs during the late modernist period follow the Ant's example with a seat and back designed as a single element.

The Ant is a clear example of the turn towards organic lines that dominated post-war art, architecture and design. In building architecture Jacobsen continued to work with straight lines and right angles. That made the laminated veneer chairs look like stabiles by Alexander Calder, and his polystyrene furniture like Henry Moore sculptures. The curvy, flowing contours of the furniture stood out in the rectilinear rooms.

Poul Kjærholm
1929–1980

Poul Kjærholm initially wanted to be an artist but completed his apprenticeship as a cabinetmaker in the Danish city of Hjørring in 1949. Next, he attended the School of Arts and Crafts in Copenhagen for three years. After graduation he taught at the school from 1952 to 1956. Kjærholm also taught at the Furniture School at the Royal Danish Academy of Fine Arts. In 1955 he began to teach at the Academy, in 1959 he made associate professor there, and in 1976 he succeeded Ole Wanscher as professor at the Furniture School.

Kjærholm's graduation project at the School of Arts and Crafts under Hans J. Wegner, an easy chair in slit flat steel and flag halyard, was so interesting in construction and materials that Wegner arranged for Kjærholm to work for the Fritz Hansen furniture factory. Here Kjærholm experimented with new materials and constructions. The prototypes were exhibited and won critical acclaim but were never put into production. Around this time, Arne Jacobsen, with inspiration from Charles Eames, designed his first three-dimensional shell chairs for Fritz Hansen, while Kjærholm was experimenting with bending the laminated veneer so dramatically that it could form legs.

Poul Kjærholm's designs were so demanding in terms of production methods and finish that not even the biggest, most modern furniture factory was able to deliver. Like Arne Jacobsen he wanted to create industrial furniture that was every bit as good as the finest handcrafted pieces. Thus, it was not until 1955, when he got in touch with the manufacturer E. Kold Christensen, via Wegner, that Kjærholm's furniture could be put into production. Kold Christensen did not have a manufacturing plant but relied on subcontractors, which allowed Kjærholm to combine the best elements of industry and craft-based production. His uncompromising perfectionism also applied to his own work. He never settled for anything less than perfect; nothing in his production was spontaneous or left to chance, everything was carefully worked through with the same attention to detail that characterised the work of Kaare Klint, the first professor at the Furniture School. As a result, Kjærholm's total output was limited.

Kjærholm has gained more world-wide recognition for his furniture than most Danish designers, and indeed, he and Arne Jacobsen had a more internationally oriented expression than most. Jacobsen's and Finn Juhl's furniture featured sculptural forms whose organic lines marked a contrast to the straight lines and clean surfaces of modernist concrete and brick architecture. Kjærholm's furniture was not intended to offer dynamic contrast to the static rooms. Instead, it appears as subordinate aspects of the architecture, echoing its straight lines, simple order, visual lightness and precise expression.

Both in form and materials, Kjærholm's furniture is closely related to Bauhaus furniture. Form and function always come together in a perfect whole marked by succinct simplicity. Like architects such as Marcel Breuer and Mies van der Rohe, Kjærholm was drawn to the possibilities of the circle, the square and the cube. And like the Bauhaus architects, Kjærholm had realised the aesthetic qualities industrialisation could bring to furniture design. Kjærholm did not turn to mass production because he felt, like the Bauhaus designers, that furniture should have a social purpose. He only drew on the artistic expression of Bauhaus, not its ideology. However, Kjærholm's desire to design simple constructions with clarified details meant that his furniture almost adhered more closely to Mies van der Rohe's dictum of 'less is more' than van der Rohe's own furniture. Just as Mies van der Rohe's strict architecture hints at classicism, Kjærholm's furniture contains elements of the version of Danish classicism that Professor Nicolai Abildgaard cultivated at the Royal Danish academy of Fine Arts during the late 18th and early 19th centuries. Kjærholm also drew on the Danish tradition in his furniture types, revisiting several of Kaare Klint's themes, including the frame chair, the deck chair and the folding stool.

Although Kjærholm, like Børge Mogensen and Hans J. Wegner, was a cabinetmaker he never designed traditional cabinetmaker's constructions, and his preferred material was steel. The chromed tubular-steel furniture of the 1930s by Poul Henningsen and Mogens Lassen, among others, was never really successful in Denmark. However, Kjærholm considered steel a natural material with the same inherent value as wood and leather. In his view, steel ages just as beautifully as organic materials with the right polish and finish. The unique advantages of steel as a structural material, its strength and springiness were properties that Kjærholm explored.

Steel was suited for making furniture that looked light and straightforward. Kjærholm's constructions are always straightforward. The functional role of each element is easily decoded, and the joints and connections are visible. The obvious and simple constructions and the exquisite and perfectly processed materials make Kjærholm's furniture both honest and exclusive. Unfortunately, production costs are too high to allow for a scale that can bring down the retail price. During the last years of his life Kjærholm focused more on wood and attempted to make a bentwood chair akin to Michael Thonet's.

Kjærholm envisioned his furniture placed in large, bright rooms with only the most essential furnishings. The furniture should be arranged in a systematic, easily decoded and open composition that was so well balanced that it felt natural and informal, despite its regularity and pre-defined structure. The room would not appear frozen or dead because the individual pieces of furniture were assigned a fixed placement or were placed at right angles to each other or in parallel rows. With their bodies and conversations, the people using the room would fil lit with life and movement, variation and colour.

Verner Panton
1926–1998

Verner Panton initially wanted to be a painter, but after completing lower secondary school in 1944 he apprenticed as a bricklayer before attending Odense Technical College, where he trained as a building technician. In 1947–1951 he attended the Royal Danish Academy of Fine Arts, School of Architecture in Copenhagen, where he studied under Kay Fisker and Erik Chr. Sørensen. After that, he attended Martin Johansen's psychology course at the University of Copenhagen, which dealt with the psychological effect of colours, space and proportions. In 1946 Panton worked for John Tommerup, in 1950 for Poul and Simon Henningsen and in 1950–1952 for Arne Jacobsen. In 1955–1962 Panton had his own studio in Denmark. In 1962 he relocated his firm to Cannes and the following year to Basel, where the firm remained until his death.

Panton is one of the most famous Danish designers, and indeed, from the beginning of his career he had a more international outlook than any other Danish designer. In 1955–1958, for example, he toured Europe to visit manufacturers. When budding Danish furniture designers such as Børge Mogensen and Hans J. Wegner visited museums to study historical chairs or found inspiration in nature, Panton visited exhibitions abroad to see the latest new developments in the emerging pop culture or examine the possibilities of innovative technologies.

From the outset, Panton knew that he did not want to pursue the Klint School's idea of cultivating the Danish rational craft tradition and its solid, aesthetically understated, harmonious furniture. In Arne Jacobsen's studio he had been involved in the development of the Ant stacking chair. He had seen the potentials of the idiom of international organic modernism and how far one could go using new technology and new materials. Panton embraced 1970s pop culture, which was an anti-rationalist rebellion against good taste and social and moral values. Panton soon grasped the informal qualities and the consumer culture of the time. He created furniture for his own time, not for eternity. In his experimental attempts at turning furniture into industrial design Panton claimed his place on the international avant-garde design scene alongside such figures as Harry Bertoia, George Nelson, Warren Platner, Joe Colombo, Pierre Paulin, Vico Magistretti and Eero Aarnio. They too worked with plastic, fibreglass, glass, Plexiglas, steel, polystyrene and synthetic textiles and used them as high-end, sophisticated materials.

Like Arne Jacobsen, Panton created total designs, but as an architect he focused almost exclusively on interior design. In his opinion, far too few architects worked with interiors. His rooms were *Gesamtkunstwerke*, total works of art, where architecture, sculpture and painting fused to create a grater whole. Colours, forms, materials, lighting and ornamentation dissolved the geometric rooms into new organic wholes.

In his interior-design commissions, which included homes, restaurants, bars, hotels, entertainment venues, offices and exhibitions, he designed furniture, textiles, light fittings and graphic art. The science-fiction-like spaces set the body free. In Panton's furniture people can lie down, lounge or virtually float in space.

The dynamic, open spatial sequences were shaped by colour. The relationship between colour, form and space had always held Panton's fascination. His use of rich, intense colours is a marked contrast to the cool, light Scandinavian tradition. He developed a palette consisting of a spectrum with 84 colours and wrote a book on the use of colours, *Lidt om Farve/Notes on Colour*. His theoretical studies on the capacity of colours to define a mood in architecture and their impact on our senses and emotions positions Panton as part of a tradition stretching back to J. W. Goethe, Wassily Kandinsky and Johannes Itten.

Both geometric and organic forms, according to Panton, had an expressive character that enhances the effect of a colour. As in contemporary concrete painting, the circle, the triangle and the square as well as the sphere, the cone and the cube were primary elements in his production. The many synthetic materials, including laminated wood, fibre, plastic and metal wire, were used in furniture pieces resembling modern, abstract sculptures that were in fact new, elegant constructions designed to support a seated or reclining body. Humour is a common element in Panton's design. Like both Arne Jacobsen and Finn Juhl, Panton always pushes the potential of his materials to the utmost. His experiments with chairs without legs resulted in cantilever constructions cast in a single piece, shell constructions on a foot or base, constructions held up by wooden boards or steel frames, with or without padding, iron grid furniture or furniture shaped in polystyrene.

Literature

Good introductions to Danish furniture design and furniture designers from the 20th century:

Andresen, Carl Erik: Dansk Møbelindustri 1870-1950. [Danish Furniture Industry 1870-1950]. Systime, Århus 1996.

Dalby, Mette Strømgaard: Stolen. [The Chair]. Trapholt/Gad, Copenhagen 2009.

Dybdahl, Lars: The Danish Furniture Boom 1945-1975. Strandberg Publishing, Copenhagen 2017.

Dybdahl, Lars; Engholm, Ida (eds.): Design: Stolen. [Design: The Chair]. Gyldendal, Copenhagen 2009.

Engholm, Ida; Michelsen, Anders: Verner Panton – environments, colours, systems, patterns. Strandberg Publishing, Copenhagen 2017.

Esbjørn, Hjort: Finn Juhl. Danish Architectural Press, Copenhagen 2001.

Gelfer-Jørgensen, Mirjam (ed.): Herculanum på Sjælland, klassicisme og nyantik i dansk møbeltradition. [Herculanum on Zealand, classicism and neo-antiquity in the Danish furniture tradition]. Rhodos, Copenhagen 1988.

Gelfer-Jørgensen, Mirjam: Danish Neo-Antique Furniture: From Abildgaard to Kaare Klint. Museum Tusculanums Forlag, Copenhagen 2017.

Hansen, Per H.: Danish Modern Furniture 1930-2016. The Rise, Decline and Re-emergence of a Cultural Market Category. Syddansk Universitetsforlag 2018.

Hansen, Per H.: Finn Juhl and His House. Strandberg Publishing, Copenhagen, 2014.

Jalk, Grete: Dansk møbelkunst gennem 40 aar: Københavns Snedkerlaugs Møbeludstillinger 1927-1966 = 40 Years of Danish Furniture Design: The Copenhagen Cabinetmakers' Guild Exhibitions 1927-1966. Teknologisk Instituts Forlag, Copenhagen 1987.

Harkjær, Gorm: Kaare Klint. Forlaget Klintiana, Copenhagen 2010.

Kaiser, Birgit: Den ideologiske funktionalisme. [Idelogical functionalism]. Gad, Copenhagen 1992.

Karlsen, Arne: Danish Furniture Design in the 20th Century, vols. 1-2. Christian Ejlers, Copenhagen 2007.

Laursen, Bodil Busk; Matz, Søren; Olesen, Christian Holmsted: Mesterværker – 100 års dansk møbelsnedkeri. Nyt Nordisk Forlag, Copenhagen 2000.

Müller, Michael: Børge Mogensen – Simplicity and Function. Hatje Cantz, Berlin/Stuttgart 2017.

Olesen, Christian Holmsted: Hans J. Wegner: Just One Good Chair. Hatje Cantz, Berlin/Stuttgart 2014.

Sheridan, Michael: Poul Kjærholm – Furniture Architect. Louisiana Museum of Modern Art, Copenhagen 2006.

Sheridan, Michael: The Furniture of Poul Kjærholm – Catalogue Raisonné. Gregory R. Miller & Co., New York 2007.

Sommer, Anne-Louise: Watercolors by Finn Juhl. Strandberg Publishing, Copenhagen 2015.

Thau, Carsten; Vindum, Kjeld: Arne Jacobsen. Second edition. Danish Architectural Press, Copenhagen 2002.

Tøjner, Poul Erik (ed.): Store danske designere. [Important Danish Designers] Lindhardt og Ringhof, Copenhagen 2008.

Wanscher, Ole: Møbeltyper. Aschehoug, Copenhagen 1932.

Wanscher, Ole: Møblets æstetik: formernes forvandling. Danish Architectural Press, Copenhagen 1985.

The Danish Chair – an International Affair
© 2018, 2024 Christian Holmsted Olesen and
Strandberg Publishing

Text contributions: Peniila Anastasia Laviolette
and Sidsel Vogdrup-Schmidt
Editing: Hanne Rask

Project management: Sidsel Kjærulff Rasmussen
Translation: Annemette Fogh and Dorte Herholdt Silver
Photo editing: Sidsel Vogdrup-Schmidt and Mille Bjørnstrup
Layout and cover design: Rasmus Koch Studio
The book was typeset using Ag Book Pro
Paper: Arctic Volume White 130 g
Litho: Narayana Press, Gylling
Printing: PNB Print

Printed in Latvia, 2024
Second edition, first print run
ISBN: 978-87-92596-62-8

This book may only be copied at institutions which have
an agreement with Copydan, and only within the terms
of that agreement.

Strandberg Publishing A/S
Gammel Mønt 14
DK-1117 Copenhagen
Denmark
www.strandbergpublishing.dk

Image credits

With the exception of the images listed below,
the illustrations in the book were photographed
by Pernille Klemp.

Aage Lund Jensen 82, 126, 127
Aage Strüwing 263
©Bruno Mathsson International 52
Børge Mogensens Tegnestue 65, 210, 211, 329
Cassina 76, 77
Cecilie Manz 104, 105
Christina Strand 288
Designmuseum Danmark 113, 137, 158,
159, 183, 326
Hans J. Wegners Tegnestue I/S 42, 118,
119, 165, 167, 198, 280, 281
Jens Risom Archive 53
Jonals Co. 64
Jørgen Gammelgaard 29, 31
Komplot Design 289
Kritisk Revy, Dec. 1927 92, 93
Kvinderegensen 190, 191
Maarbjergs Atelier 112
Nordisk Pressefoto, Holger Damgaard
186, 187
©Panton Design, Basel 316, 317
Poul Kjærholm 46, 47, 98, 99, 249, 312, 313

Peter Johansen 298
PP Møbler 330
©Republic of Fritz Hansen 88, 89, 199,
248, 256, 262, 268, 269
Ritzau Scanpix 15, 327, 328, 332, 333, 334
The Royal Danish Library 331
Schnakenburg & Brahl Fotografi 130, 131,
173, 242
Sophus Bengtsson, Thorvaldsens
Museum 147
THONET GmbH, Germany 83
Unknown photographer 25, 27, 146, 162,
243, 257, 274, 275
Øhavsmuseet, Faaborg 142, 143

—

The editors have attempted to identify all the
licence holders for the illustrations used in the
book. If we have missed any, we kindly ask you
to contact the publisher, and you will receive
the standard fee.